**2**

The Short Essay

# EFFECTIVE
# Academic Writing

## SECOND EDITION

Alice Savage
Patricia Mayer

**OXFORD**
UNIVERSITY PRESS

# OXFORD
## UNIVERSITY PRESS

198 Madison Avenue
New York, NY 10016 USA

Great Clarendon Street, Oxford, ox2 6dp, United Kingdom

Oxford University Press is a department of the University of Oxford.
It furthers the University's objective of excellence in research, scholarship,
and education by publishing worldwide. Oxford is a registered trade
mark of Oxford University Press in the UK and in certain other countries

General Manager, American ELT: Laura Pearson
Publisher: Stephanie Karras
Associate Publishing Manager: Sharon Sargent
Managing Editor: Jennifer Meldrum
Director, ADP: Susan Sanguily
Executive Design Manager: Maj-Britt Hagsted
Associate Design Manager: Michael Steinhofer
Image Manager: Trisha Masterson
Electronic Production Manager: Julie Armstrong
Production Artist: Elissa Santos
Production Coordinator: Chris Espejo
Production Coordinator: Brad Tucker

ISBN: 978 0 19 432347 5 EFFECTIVE ACADEMIC WRITING 2 WITH ONLINE
PRACTICE PACK
ISBN: 978 0 19 432342 0 EFFECTIVE ACADEMIC WRITING 2 STUDENT BOOK AS
PACK COMPONENT
ISBN: 978 0 19 433391 7 EFFECTIVE ACADEMIC WRITING ONLINE

Printed in China

This book is printed on paper from certified and well-managed sources

ACKNOWLEDGEMENTS

*The authors and publisher are grateful to those who have given permission to reproduce
the following extracts and adaptations of copyright material:*

p. 29 From *When I Was a Puerto Rican* by Esmeralda Santiago. Copyright © 2006
Esmeralda Santiago. Reprinted by permission of Da Capo Press, a member of
the Perseus Books Group; p. 55 From "Breaking Ground to be a Man" from
*An Hour Before Daylight* by Jimmy Carter, 2001 Reprinted by permission of the
author; p. 81 From *Banker to the Poor* by Muhammad Yunus. Copyright © 2003
Muhammad Yunus. Reprinted by permission of Public Affairs, a member
of Perseus Books Group; p. 131 From "Chapter 2: Causes of Poverty and a
Framework for Action" in *World Bank Development Report 2000-2001: Attacking
Poverty* by The World Bank. Reprinted by permission of International Bank
for Reconstruction and Development/The World Bank.

*We would also like to thank the following for permission to reproduce the following
photographs:*

Cover, sebastian-julian/istockphoto.com; viii, Marcin Krygier/iStockphoto
(laptop); p. vi, Opener, Writing Process and Review pages, 152 stocksnapper/
istockphoto (letter texture); p. viii Marcin Krygier/iStockphoto; pp. 1, 2 Marka/
Alamy; p. 2 Jemal Countess/WireImage/Getty Images; pp. 27, 28 Peter
Forsberg/Alamy; pp. 50, 76, 100, 126, 156 Monkey Business Images/
Shutterstock (Clock); pp. 53, 54 Germanskydiver/Shutterstock;
p. 55 Library of Congress; pp. 79, 80 Fuse/Getty Images; p. 80 Alamy;
pp. 103, 104 Alan Becker/The Image Bank/Getty Images;
pp. 129, 130 SCPhotos/Alamy; p. 130 The Print Collector/Alamy.

# Reviewers

*We would like to acknowledge the following individuals for their input during the development of the series:*

**Chris Alexis**, College of Applied Sciences, Sur, Oman

**Amina Saif Mohammed Al Hashamia**, College of Applied Sciences, Nizwa, Oman

**Amal Al Muqarshi**, College of Applied Sciences, Ibri, Oman

**Saleh Khalfan Issa Al-Rahbi**, College of Applied Sciences, Nizwa, Oman

**Dr. Debra Baldwin**, UPP, Alfaisal University, Saudi Arabia

**Virginia L. Bouchard**, George Mason University, English Language Institute, Washington D.C.

**Judith Buckman**, College of Applied Sciences, Salalah, Oman

**Dr. Catherine Buon**, American University of Armenia, Armenia

**Mei-Rong Alice Chen**, National Taiwan University of Science and Technology, Taipei

**Mark L. Cummings**, Jefferson Community and Technical College, KY

**Hitoshi Eguchi**, Hokusei Gakuen University, Japan

**Elizabeth W. Foss**, Washtenaw Community College, MI

**Sally C. Gearhart**, Santa Rosa Junior College, CA

**Alyona Gorokhova**, Miramar Community College, CA

**Dr. Simon Green**, College of Applied Sciences, Oman

**Janis Hearn**, Hongik University, South Korea

**Adam Henricksen**, University of Maryland, Baltimore County, MD

**Clay Hindman**, Sierra College, CA

**Kuei-ping Vicky Hsu**, National Tsing Hua University, Hsinchu

**Azade Johnson**, Abu Dhabi Men's College, Higher Colleges of Technology, U.A.E.

**Chandra Johnson**, Fresno Pacific University, CA

**Pei-Lun Kao**, Chang Gung University, Gueishan

**Yuko Kobayashi**, Tokyo University of Science, Japan

**Blair Lee**, Kyung Hee University, Japan

**Chia-yu Lin**, National Tsing Hua University, Hsinchu

**Kent McClintock**, Chosun University, South Korea

**Joan Oakley**, College of the North Atlantic-Qatar, Qatar

**Fernanda G. Ortiz**, CESL University of Arizona, AZ

**William D. Phelps**, Southern Illinois University, IL

**Dorothy Ramsay**, College of Applied Sciences, Sohar, Oman

**Vidya Rangachari**, Mission College, CA

**Elizabeth Rasmussen**, Northern Virginia Community College, VA

**Syl Rice**, Abu Dhabi Men's College, Higher Colleges of Technology, U.A.E.

**Donna Schaeffer**, University of Washington, WA

**Dr. Catherine Schaff-Stump**, Kirkwood Community College, IA

**Mary-Jane Scott**, Sungshin Women's University, South Korea

**Jenay Seymour**, Hong-ik University, South Korea

**Janet Sloan Rachidi**, U.A.E. University, Al Ain, U.A.E.

**Bob Studholme**, U.A.E. University, Al Ain, U.A.E.

**Paula Suzuki**, SI-UK Language Centre, Japan

**Sabine Thépaut**, Intensive English Language Institute, University of North Texas, TX

**Shu-Hui Yu**, Ling Tung University, Taichung

## Author Acknowledgments

Our most profound appreciation goes to Sharon Sargent for adding her vision and improving this book, to Vicky Aeschbacher for her generous, patient, and meticulous editorial skills, and to Alex Regan and Jennifer Meldrum for their attention to detail. We'd also like to thank our families for their continuous love and support.

P.M. and A.S.

# Contents

| Unit | Academic Focus | Rhetorical Focus | Language and Grammar Focus |
|------|----------------|------------------|----------------------------|
| **5**<br><br>**Opinion Essays**<br><br>page 103 | **Technology** | • Opinion organization<br>• Facts and opinions<br>• Counter-argument and refutation | • Quantity expressions in opinion essays<br>• Connectors to show support and opposition |
| **6**<br><br>**Cause-and-Effect Essays**<br><br>page 129 | **Education and Economics** | • Cause-and-effect organization<br>• Clustering information | • Phrasal verbs<br>• The future with *will*<br>• *Will* with *so that*<br>• Future possibilities with *if* clauses |

# Welcome to Effective Academic Writing

*Effective Academic Writing, Second Edition* instills student confidence and provides the tools necessary for successful academic writing.

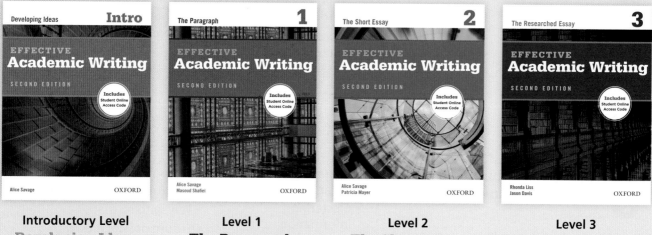

**Introductory Level**
**Developing Ideas**

**Level 1**
**The Paragraph**

**Level 2**
**The Short Essay**

**Level 3**
**The Researched Essay**

- Step-by-step **Writing Process** guides and refines writing skills.

- **Timed writing** practice prepares students for success on high-stakes tests.

- **Online Writing Tutor** improves academic writing inside and outside the classroom.

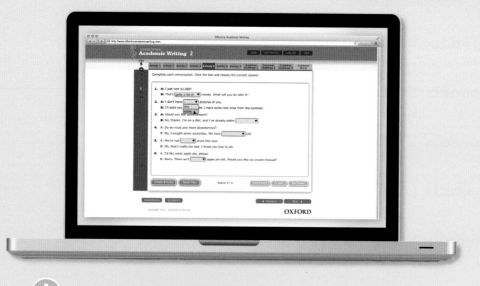

 **Online Writing Support for all Levels**

# Overview

## *Effective Academic Writing, Second Edition* delivers practice that will improve your students' writing.

- NEW! The new **Introductory Level** provides students with the support and instruction they need for writing success in the lowest-level writing courses.
- NEW! **More content-area related assignments** with more academic vocabulary and readings prepare students for the challenges of the academic classroom.

**Writing Process Step 1** Stimulating Ideas

**Writing Process Step 2** Brainstorming and Outlining

**Writing Process Step 3** Developing Your Ideas

**Writing Process Step 4** Editing Your Writing

Each unit introduces an academic content theme and writing task and guides students through the **Writing Process**.

### Rhetorical Focus

**Narrative Organization**
A **narrative** is a story. It has an introduction that engages the reader's interest, details about the main event or action in the story, and a conclusion that describes the outcome.

**Introduction**
- The hook gets the reader's attention.
- The middle sentences introduce an event (the action of the story) by providing background information about the people, the place, and the time.
- The thesis statement prepares the reader for the action that follows.

**Body Paragraphs**
- The body paragraphs describe what happened in the story.
- They include details that bring the story to life.
- They often use time order to explain the event.

**Conclusion**
- A conclusion describes the outcome of the event.
- Narrative essays often end with a comment about the event's importance in the writer's life.

Each unit addresses a particular rhetorical mode and provides **user-friendly guidance** to help students master the form.

**Concise and effective language and grammar presentations** develop students' understanding and improve their accuracy.

### Language and Grammar Focus

GO ONLINE

**Using the Past Continuous in Narrative Essays**
In a narrative, you often need to describe actions in progress or to describe background actions.

To form the **past continuous**, use *was/were* and the base form of the verb + *-ing*.

Use the past continuous to talk about activities that were in progress at a specific time in the past. The activities began before the specific time and may also have continued after that time.

At three o'clock we **were walking** home from school. My friend was **riding** his bicycle.

Also use the past continuous to describe background actions.

The sun **was going** down, and the children **were** still **playing** on the grass.

We don't usually use stative verbs (*be, know, own, mean, seem, understand, love, believe, etc.*) in the past continuous. We use the simple past instead.

I **didn't know** John then.

X   I wasn't knowing John then. (INCORRECT)

**Timed Writing** | Preparing for Academic Success

**Timed writing** prepares students for exams and high-stakes tests.

# Effective Academic Writing **Online**

**IT'S EASY!** Use the access code printed on the inside back cover of this book to register at www.effectiveacademicwriting.com.

**GO ONLINE**

## For the Student

- *Online Writing Tutor* helps students retain and apply their writing skills.
  - Models of the unit writing assignments **demonstrate good writing** and allow students to understand how each text is constructed.
  - **Writing frameworks help students with organizing and structuring,** for the sentence level, paragraph level, and the text as a whole.
  - Students can plan, structure, and write their own texts, check their work, **then save, print, or send directly to their teacher.**

- Extensive **Online Grammar Practice** and **grammar term glossary** support students in using grammar structures appropriately and fluently in their writing.

- Comprehensive **Peer Editor's Checklists** support collaborative learning.

- **Printable Outline Templates** support the writing process.

## For the Teacher

- **IELTS-style, TOEFL-style, and TOEIC-style online writing tests** can be **customized** and **printed.**

- **Online test rubrics** make grading easy.

- **Online Grammar Practice** is automatically graded and entered into the online grade book.

- Answer keys makes grading easy.

- The **online management system** allows you to manage your classes. View, print, or export all class and student reports.

> **FOR ADDITIONAL SUPPORT**
> Email our customer support team at eltsupport@oup.com.

> **FOR TEACHER CODES**
> Please contact your sales representative for a **Teacher Access Code.** Teacher Access Codes are sold separately.

viii   Introduction

# 1

# Paragraph to Short Essay

## Unit Goals

### Rhetorical Focus

- paragraph structure
- the topic sentence
- unity and coherence
- the paragraph and the short essay
- short essay organization

### Language and Grammar Focus

- simple and compound sentences
- run-on sentences
- dependent clauses

"Writing is one of the most solitary activities in the world." — **Paulo Coelho**

"I write entirely to find out what I'm thinking, what I'm looking at, what I see and what it means. What I want and what I fear." — **Joan Didion**

## Exercise 1  Thinking about the topic

A. Read the quotes about writing. Why do these professional authors write? Do you share their feelings in any way?

B. Now discuss the quotes in small groups. Make notes about your feelings on writing. As a group, present your views on writing.

### Rhetorical Focus

#### Review of Paragraph Structure

A **paragraph** is a group of sentences about a topic. A typical paragraph begins with a **topic sentence,** which introduces the topic. The sentences that follow support the idea in the topic sentence with explanations, reasons, and other details. The **concluding sentence** brings the paragraph to an end.

#### Formatting a Paragraph

• Leave one-inch margins on the left and right side of the page.

• Indent the first sentence. The rest of the sentences follow each other, so that the paragraph looks like a square with a little space taken out of the corner.

• Double-space your paragraph.

## Exercise 2 Identifying the elements of a student paragraph

**A. Read the paragraph. Then label the formatting elements of the paragraph. Use the letters in the box.**

| | | |
|---|---|---|
| a. double spacing | b. margin | c. indent |

### The Ice-Man

1. ____ ⟶       Whenever I remember my experience in flight school, I think
of my instructor because he taught me how to fly a jet. His nickname
was Ice-Man because he was always calm. This was a positive

2. ____ ⟵⟶ characteristic because he had to teach students not to panic in
a dangerous situation. For example, one time, I made a big mistake

3. ____ ⟨ while we were flying in the clouds. Most instructors would take control
and fix the situation, but not Ice-Man. He just gave instructions to fix the
problem. I corrected the mistake and gained confidence in my abilities.
I will always remember his quiet, clear voice and the black aviator
glasses that he wore. He was a special person in my life, and I hope that
someday I will see him again and thank him for helping me to realize my
dream of flying solo and becoming a real pilot.

**B. Answer the questions about the paragraph above. Give reasons for your answers.**

1. Circle the topic sentence. Does the topic sentence help you understand what the paragraph will be about?

   _____

2. How many supporting sentences does the paragraph have? Underline them.

   _____

3. Do all the supporting sentences relate to the topic sentence?

   _____

4. Circle the concluding sentence. Does the concluding sentence make the paragraph feel finished?

   _____

## Exercise 3 Reading a student paragraph

**Read the paragraph. What risk did the boy take?**

# The Coconut Tree

When I was a boy and first learning about the world, I took a big risk. I was playing in the yard outside of my family's house with my friends. It was a hot day, and we were resting in the shady side of our house. One of my friends dared me to climb the coconut tree in our yard. I looked at the tree. It was mature and very tall but a little bit curved. I had seen men climbing these trees, and it looked easy, but I had never tried before. I wanted to show my courage, so I said I would. The tree was scratchy, but I found places for my feet and hands, and soon I was near the top. But then the tree began to move in the breeze. Suddenly I fell. There was a great pain in my arm. My friends ran to tell my mother. She took me to the hospital. I had a broken arm, and one of my ribs was broken. I felt bad for a long time after that. The worst part was that every day I had to walk past the coconut tree and remember my foolish risk.

## Exercise 4 Examining the student paragraph

**A. Examine the paragraph by responding to the questions and statements below.**

1. Underline the topic sentence. Is it the first or second sentence? _____

2. Is the first sentence indented? _____

3. How many supporting sentences are there? Which are they? _____

4. Circle the concluding sentence.

**B. Respond to the paragraph by answering the following questions.**

1. Where was the writer at the time of the event? _____

2. Who was he with? _____

3. What was the consequence of the risk he took? _____

    _____

4. Have you ever done something risky? What? _____

    _____

## The Topic Sentence

An effective paragraph contains a good **topic sentence.** A successful topic sentence has the following features.

- It introduces the topic, or what the paragraph will be about. It also contains an idea or opinion about the topic. This idea is called a **controlling idea.**

    Certain types of **insects** <u>can benefit a garden</u>.

- The topic sentence must not be a simple fact or detail. Instead, it must contain a specific idea. The idea or opinion must not be too general, or the topic sentence will be unclear.

    There are approximately 4,000 chemicals in cigarette smoke. *(fact, not topic sentence)*

    Smoking is bad. *(idea, too general for a topic sentence)*

    Smoking advertisements have a harmful influence on children. *(specific idea)*

- The topic sentence usually appears as the first or second sentence of a paragraph. Here it is the second sentence.

    Have you ever noticed that closets are getting bigger and rooms are getting smaller? <u>Changes in popular culture can be seen in changes to the typical family home.</u>

- The topic sentence implies the purpose of the paragraph: to explain, narrate, compare, describe, explain causes or effects, demonstrate, argue, or provide the steps in a process.

    My sister's personality is completely different from mine. *(shows comparison)*

    Smoking results in thousands of smoking-related deaths each year. *(tells cause and effect)*

## Exercise 5 Identifying topics and controlling ideas

**Circle the topic, and underline the controlling idea in the topic sentences below.**

1. The painting *Starry Night* by Vincent van Gogh is fascinating in many ways.

2. My first driving lesson was a disaster.

3. The process of getting a driver's license has several steps.

4. My ability to speak English has changed my life in several important ways.

5. Some computer games involve the player in physical activity.

6. Cloudy weather affects certain people in negative ways.

## Exercise 6 Identifying purpose in topic sentences

**Identify the purpose of the paragraph that follows logically from each topic sentence below.**

1. Almost anyone can get a good grade if they follow these instructions.
   a. express an opinion    b. tell steps in a process    c. narrate a story

2. There are three major causes of obesity in children.
   a. compare two subjects    b. explain causes and effects    c. describe a topic

3. I will always remember a fishing trip that I took with my father when I was 12 years old.
   a. compare two subjects    b. explain causes and effects    c. narrate a story

4. I believe that students should not own credit cards.
   a. tell steps in a process    b. explain causes and effects    c. express an opinion

5. Owls are different from hawks in several significant ways.
   a. compare two subjects    b. describe a topic    c. express an opinion

## Exercise 7 Predicting paragraphs from controlling ideas

**Circle the topic and underline the controlling idea of each topic sentence below. Then with a partner, predict what the rest of the paragraph will discuss.**

1. Immigrating to Canada from Vietnam was difficult for my parents.

   **Prediction:** _A narrative about the writer's parents' journey from Vietnam to Canada._

2. Cell phones should not be allowed in classrooms for several reasons.

   **Prediction:** _____

   _____

3. Cancún Restaurant has the best seafood in town.

   **Prediction:** _____

   _____

4. Training for the marathon is a complicated process.

   **Prediction:** _____

   _____

5. Taking the TOEFL test is a hardship for many students.

   **Prediction:** _____

   _____

## Exercise 8 Identifying effective topic sentences

**Read each pair of sentences. Write *TS* next to the sentence that is more effective. Be prepared to explain your choice.**

1. _TS_ a. An English-English dictionary is the best choice for English learners.
   _____ b. Many English learners use dictionaries.

2. _____ a. The grains of rice should not stick together.
   _____ b. Persian rice is only considered authentic if it is made in the following way.

3. _____ a. The Internet has changed the way students do research for term papers.
   _____ b. The Internet is changing students' lives.

4. _____ a. A college degree is important.
   _____ b. Having a college degree has many positive effects on a person's life.

## Exercise 9 Writing effective topic sentences

**For each question, choose two of the purposes below and write a topic sentence for each.**

**Purposes**

| | | |
|---|---|---|
| compare two topics | explain effects | tell a story |
| describe something | give an opinion | tell steps in a process |
| explain causes | | |

1. Soccer
   a. **Purpose:** _to explain the positive effects of playing soccer._

   **Topic Sentence:** _Playing soccer offers many benefits._

   _____

   b. **Purpose:** _to compare soccer and basketball as a way to inform people._

   **Topic Sentence:** _Soccer and basketball look different, but they have_

   _many similarities._

2. A wedding
   a. **Purpose:** _____

   **Topic Sentence:** _____

   _____

   b. **Purpose:** _____

   **Topic Sentence:** _____

   _____

3. An adventure
   a. **Purpose:** _____

   **Topic Sentence:** _____

   _____

   b. **Purpose:** _____

   **Topic Sentence:** _____

   _____

4. Fear
   a. **Purpose:** _____

   **Topic Sentence:** _____

   _____

   b. **Purpose:** _____

   **Topic Sentence:** _____

   _____

5. Desserts
   a. **Purpose:** _____

   **Topic Sentence:** _____

   _____

   b. **Purpose:** _____

   **Topic Sentence:** _____

   _____

 In **Writing Process Part 2** you will . . .

- learn about paragraph unity and coherence.

## Rhetorical Focus 🔍

### Unity within a Paragraph

Effective writing must have **unity.** A paragraph has unity when all the sentences support one single idea.

The paragraph must have one controlling idea in the topic sentence. Otherwise, the paragraph loses focus.

The supporting sentences must support, demonstrate, prove, or develop the main idea in the topic sentence. If they do not, they will be irrelevant or off-topic and destroy the unity of the paragraph.

The concluding sentence should restate the idea in the topic sentence to reinforce the main idea for the reader.

## Exercise 1  Reading a student paragraph

Read the paragraph. What is the talent of each of the three family members described in the paragraph?

## Stories of Nepal

My mother grew up in a creative and interesting family in Nepal. Her father was an astronomer who worked for the King of Nepal. Very often my grandfather would take my mother to work with him so she could look through a telescope and see the planets and stars. Then she would play in the planetarium until her older brother came to pick her up. On the walk home, her brother would tell her stories. Sometimes he would point to someone on the street or standing in a doorway and begin a new story about the person. My grandmother was also interesting. She liked to paint portraits of children. She painted many beautiful portraits of my mother although my mother said it was difficult to sit still. After my mother left Nepal, she studied computer programming in Wisconsin. I love to remember my mother's stories, and now I enjoy telling my own daughter about her grandmother's life in Nepal.

## Exercise 2 Examining the student paragraph for unity

Examine the organization of the paragraph by responding to the following questions and statements. Then compare your answers with a partner.

1. Underline the topic sentence. Is it the first or second sentence? _____

2. Write the controlling idea from the topic sentence in your own words.

   _____

   _____

3. One sentence in the paragraph is irrelevant. Draw a line through it.

4. Why is the sentence irrelevant? Write your explanation below.

   _____

   _____

## Exercise 3 Recognizing unity in supporting sentences

Read the following topic sentences. Put a check (✓) next to each sentence below that supports the topic sentence.

1. There are several reasons why online courses are increasing in popularity.
   - ✓ a. Online courses are flexible in terms of time.
   - _____ b. Online courses have been available since the 1990s.
   - ✓ c. Online courses are more convenient for students who live far away from the campus.

2. Childhood diabetes has many possible causes.
   - _____ a. Obesity is a major cause of diabetes.
   - _____ b. Children who eat too much sugar can get diabetes.
   - _____ c. Children with diabetes need constant medical care.

3. The best way to reduce traffic in our city is to build a metro subway system.
   - _____ a. Pollution is very bad in our city.
   - _____ b. Widening the freeways has not solved the problem of traffic congestion.
   - _____ c. A metro subway system would encourage people to take public transportation to work.

4. I am afraid of dogs because I had a scary experience with one when I was ten.
   - _____ a. There are many dogs in the streets of my town.
   - _____ b. I was teasing the dog by moving its food.
   - _____ c. The dog bit me.

5. Scenic Beach is my favorite picnic spot because of its beauty.

   _____ a. It is a quiet, narrow beach covered with oyster shells.

   _____ b. One time I had an interesting experience there.

   _____ c. The Olympic Mountains rise straight up out of the water on the other side of the channel.

6. Train stations are interesting places to visit.

   _____ a. The architecture of each train station is often connected to the history of a city.

   _____ b. The passengers are frequently more interesting to watch than other types of travelers.

   _____ c. Trains are a good alternative for people who are afraid of flying.

7. The world of dinosaurs is very familiar to the general population.

   _____ a. Scientists believe that the birds of today are descended from dinosaurs.

   _____ b. Every year, new movies and TV shows about dinosaurs are produced.

   _____ c. Children study dinosaurs and play with dinosaur toys from an early age.

## Exercise 4 Editing for unity

**Read the paragraph. Draw a line through the sentences that are irrelevant. The first one is done for you. Find three more.**

I love to watch the pelicans in Galveston. I usually go in the winter. ~~The weather is not warm enough for swimming, so I usually do not see many people on the beach.~~ Pelicans are not elegant, but they are interesting to watch. They remind me of prehistoric birds from my school textbook on dinosaurs. I studied dinosaurs a lot when I was young, and I am very fond of them. The pelicans have large grayish-brown wings that bend sharply when they are flying, and their beaks are long, so their faces look peculiar and old. My brother also really likes pelicans. They are also graceful in their own way. A flock of pelicans will fly along the coastline just outside the waves, and when they see a good fishing spot, they stop, then turn, and dive straight down into the water. Sometimes there is an oil rig or a cargo ship in the water, too. Sometimes several pelicans will fish in the same spot for a while before moving down the beach and out of sight.

Write two or three supporting sentences for each of the following topic sentences. Then exchange books with a partner and check your partner's sentences for unity.

1. Joining a sports team can provide many benefits. _____

   _____

   _____

   _____

2. My first day in my new school was full of surprises. _____

   _____

   _____

   _____

3. A road trip is the best way to see the country. _____

   _____

   _____

   _____

4. Many people do not realize that packing a suitcase requires skill and planning.

   _____

   _____

   _____

## Rhetorical Focus

### Coherence in a Paragraph

**Coherence** in a paragraph means that the ideas have a logical flow: the relationship between the sentences is clear, and one idea connects to the next. One way to achieve coherence in a paragraph is to use a pattern of organization, such as **time order, spatial order,** or **order of importance.** To use time order, tell what happened first, next, and last. Spatial order is useful for describing items from top to bottom or from side to side. Paragraphs organized by order of importance might give the most important ideas first or leave them for last.

## Exercise 6 Reading a student paragraph

**Read the paragraph. How many rules does the writer give?**

### Important Rules for Acting on Stage

For people who would like to act in the theater, there are several important rules to remember. One rule is to make sure you face your audience when you are on stage. If you turn away from the audience, they cannot see your facial expressions. The next rule is that you must make sure that you speak loudly enough. If your audience has difficulty hearing you, they will quickly lose interest. Another important point is to memorize your lines. Rehearse them often—on the train, in the mirror, or while you are walking to class—so that you remember them. Perhaps the most important rule of all is to remain calm on stage if you forget your lines. Don't panic and stop speaking because the audience will notice. Instead, make up something to say until you remember your next line. As long as you continue speaking and appear relaxed, the audience will probably not realize that you have made a mistake. In conclusion, following these rules will help ensure a successful stage performance.

## Exercise 7 Examining the student paragraph for coherence

**Examine the organization of the paragraph by responding to the questions and statements below. Then compare your answers with a partner.**

1. Underline the topic sentence.

2. What should an actor do if he forgets his lines? _____

   _____

   _____

3. The writer uses order of importance as a pattern of organization. Do the ideas in the paragraph move from more important to less important or less important to more important?

   _____

   _____

## Exercise 8 Reordering for coherence

**Read the sentences from a narrative paragraph. Some of the sentences are out of order. Number the sentences 1–10 to show logical time order. Then compare your answers with a partner.**

_____ a. My family hugged me and cried because I had been gone so long.

__1__ b. I will never forget one day when I had to travel alone on the subway.

_____ c. I was sick, and I had to go to an appointment at the hospital.

_____ d. When my appointment ended, I got on the subway to go home.

_____ e. That was why my surroundings looked unfamiliar.

_____ f. My appointment was at 1:00 p.m.

_____ g. Suddenly I looked up and did not know where I was.

_____ h. I was exhausted and fell asleep on my way home.

_____ i. Then I realized that I had fallen asleep.

_____ j. It took me five more hours to get back to my home.

## In **Writing Process Part 3** you will . . .

- learn about short essay structure and organization.
- practice writing a thesis statement.

## Rhetorical Focus

### The Paragraph and the Short Essay

A **short essay** is longer than a paragraph, but like a paragraph it has three basic parts: an **introduction,** a **body,** and a **conclusion.**

### Introduction

- The introductory paragraph is the first paragraph of a short essay. It contains a topic sentence and **thesis statement.**

### Body Paragraphs

- A short essay has at least one or two body paragraphs. These develop the idea presented in the introduction.

### Conclusion

- The concluding paragraph is the final paragraph. It summarizes the idea(s) presented in the short essay.

Compare the similar ways that a paragraph and a short essay function.

| Paragraph | | Short Essay |
|---|---|---|
| The topic sentence states the topic. | ⟶ | The introductory paragraph states the topic. |
| The topic sentence states the the controlling idea. | ⟶ | The thesis statement states the controlling idea. |
| The supporting sentences of the paragraph support the idea in the topic sentence. | ⟶ | The body paragraphs support the idea in the thesis statement. Each body paragraph has a topic sentence. |
| The concluding sentence summarizes the idea in the topic sentence. | ⟶ | The essay conclusion summarizes the idea in the thesis statement. |

Read the paragraph and then the short essay. Which is more interesting?

## Paragraph

My uncle Patricio is one of the most interesting people in my family. He is old and has a wrinkled face. In his wallet he carries a small piece of paper that says "Remember me." Patricio has an intriguing history. He and my mother were born in a small village in the mountains. When he was 17, he left home to explore the world. Now he fixes air conditioners in Los Angeles, and during the winter months, he sometimes comes to visit us and play the accordion. I love spending time with my uncle Patricio because he has an interesting look and a mysterious past. Someday, I hope that he will tell me more about his life.

## Short Essay

My family is full of happy, crazy, and talented people. My aunt Margarita has a yard full of gorgeous plants. My brother José is an expert tailor, and my mother loves to experiment in the kitchen. However, I think the most interesting is my mysterious uncle Patricio.    **introduction**

Patricio is an elderly man with white hair sticking up all over his head. Beneath his messy hair, he has a wrinkled brown face and powerful dark eyes that show many emotions. Patricio is tall and skinny, and he wears baggy pants and plaid shirts. In his wallet he carries a small piece of paper. Written on the piece of paper are the words "Remember me." He has never told me who wrote it, or who it is from.    **body paragraph 1**

Patricio has an intriguing history. He and my mother were born in a small village in the mountains. When he was 17, he left home to explore the world. On one trip, he went to Siberia to look for gold. On another trip, he went to Alaska to work on a fishing boat. Now he fixes air conditioners in Los Angeles, and during the winter months, he sometimes comes to visit us and play the accordion.    **body paragraph 2**

I love spending time with my uncle Patricio. He has an interesting look and a sad and mysterious past. He is also a talented musician. Someday, I hope that he will tell me the story of the piece of paper and who wanted to be remembered.    **conclusion**

**Examine the paragraph and short essay by responding to the questions and statements below. Compare your answers with a partner.**

1. What information is included in the short essay introduction that is not in the topic sentence of the paragraph?

   _____

   _____

2. Circle the topic and controlling idea of body paragraph 1 in the essay.

3. What new details have been added to body paragraph 1 in the essay?

   _____

   _____

4. Circle the topic and controlling idea of body paragraph 2 in the essay.

5. What additional details have been added to body paragraph 2 in the essay?

   _____

   _____

6. What information is included in the essay conclusion that is not in the concluding sentence of the paragraph?

   _____

   _____

## Rhetorical Focus

### Short Essay Organization

An effective essay must have the following elements.

**Introduction**

- A hook is an opening sentence that attracts the reader's attention.

- The sentences after the hook give background information that helps the reader understand the topic.

- The last sentence in the introduction, the thesis statement, is very important because it gives the topic and the controlling idea of the entire essay.

**Body Paragraphs**

- An essay has at least one body paragraph in which the writer develops the thesis statement from the introduction. The body paragraph begins with a topic sentence, followed by supporting details.

**Conclusion**

- An essay ends with a conclusion that summarizes or restates the main idea in the thesis statement.

## Exercise 3 Understanding thesis statements

**A. Read the short essay. The thesis statement is missing. Choose the best thesis statement from the list following the essay. Discuss your choice with a partner.**

Imagine having a job that fits your class schedule. You do not have conflicts with studying because you only work at night and on the weekends. In addition, you can work in a beautiful room with paintings on the walls, candlelight, and soothing music playing in the background.

_____

_____

First, restaurant work is a great job for full-time students because the hours are different. Most restaurants are busiest during the weekends or in the evenings. Since students have to go to class during the week and during the day, a restaurant job is an excellent option that gives students time for class.

The second reason why restaurant work suits students is that students can eat at the restaurant. Most students are short on time. They don't have time to go shopping, cook, and clean up, so they need to get meals in a hurry. It is perfect if they can eat at work.

Students can make money, eat, and still have time for class if they work in a restaurant. For this reason, many restaurants are staffed by students. It's a great job for those who need to work while they are in college.

a. A restaurant job is a convenient choice for a college student for several reasons.
b. Many restaurants hire college students.
c. A college student can make a lot of money working in an expensive restaurant.

B. **Now read this short essay. The thesis statement is missing. Write a thesis statement on the lines provided. Make sure your thesis states a topic and a controlling idea. Compare your answer with a partner.**

I have many wonderful memories of my childhood in El Salvador, but I have one memory that still makes me shiver when I think about it. I lived with my grandmother in a house in the country, and I had many cousins to play with. The neighbors all knew me, and we children always felt safe. _____

_____

My scary experience happened when I was about ten. I was playing hide-and-seek with some children from the neighborhood when my cousin and I discovered a dark abandoned warehouse. We were happy because we thought that no one would find us there. We went inside. There were boxes, and everything was covered with dust. Suddenly my cousin ran away. I thought she was hiding, so I laughed and called her name, but she did not answer. I started to hide, too, but at that moment, I smelled a terrible odor. I looked in the corner, and a big shape was moving. It was dark, and I couldn't see very well, but I knew it was big. I ran outside. My cousin was outside, and we ran back to our house as fast as we could.

I still do not know what was in the warehouse. My grandmother said she thought some thieves had been hiding there. She said it was a good thing that they didn't see me. Her words made me more afraid. I thought, "What if they had caught me?" After that, I decided to stay away from that dark warehouse. I learned to be very careful and never go into empty buildings again, no matter what!

 In **Writing Process Part 4** you will . . .

- learn about simple and compound sentences.
- learn how to correct run-on sentences.
- learn about main and dependent clauses.

Editing involves making changes to your writing to improve it and to correct mistakes.

## Language and Grammar Focus

### The Sentence

A **sentence** contains at least one **subject** (a noun or a phrase) and a **verb,** and it expresses a complete idea. The verb expresses the action of the sentence, and the subject tells who or what completed the action. A **simple sentence** may contain more than one noun or verb.

| Subject | Verb |
|---------|------|
| The **dog** | **runs**. |
| The **dog** | **runs** and **chases** squirrels. *(two verbs)* |
| The **dog** and **cat** | **run** after squirrels. *(two nouns in subject)* |

A complete sentence must contain at least one **main clause.** A main clause contains a subject and a verb, and it expresses a complete idea.

### The Simple Sentence

A simple sentence, shown below, contains one main clause.

| Subject | Verb |
|---------|------|
| The **dog** | **runs** after squirrels. |

### The Compound Sentence

A **compound sentence** has two main clauses, separated by a **comma** and a **conjunction,** or by a **semicolon.**

| Main Clause | Conjunction | Main Clause |
|-------------|-------------|-------------|
| The dog runs after squirrels, | **and** | the squirrels run away. |
| The dog terrifies the squirrels, | **so** | they stay high in the trees. |
| The dog chases them every day, | **but** | it has never caught one. |
| The squirrels climb trees, | **or** | they run through fences. |

| Main Clause | | Main Clause |
|-------------|--|-------------|
| The dog is very agile; | | it can move quickly. |

## Exercise 1 Identifying clauses

**Read the sentences. Then circle the number of clauses contained in each sentence.**

1. The fish were hungry.                                      ① 2
2. The fish were hungry, and they ate the food quickly.        1   2
3. I love to go to the park, so I try to go every weekend.     1   2
4. The bus takes a long time, but it is less expensive than a car.  1   2
5. Computers are very important today; they can do many things.  1   2
6. My father is a man with a good education and an honest character.  1   2

## Language and Grammar Focus

### Run-on Sentences

A **run-on sentence** is not a correct sentence. In a run-on sentence, important punctuation is missing between the clauses. The sentence "runs on" too long and confuses the reader.

You can correct run-on sentences with a period, a comma and conjunction, or a semicolon.

  x  The dog runs fast it likes to chase animals in the park. (INCORRECT)
     The dog runs fast. **It** likes to chase animals in the park.
     The dog runs fast, and it likes to chase animals in the park.

  x  My little brother is difficult to take care of still I love him very much. (INCORRECT)
     My little brother is difficult to take care of; still, I love him very much.
     My little brother means a lot to me; he is my best friend.

## Exercise 2 Correcting run-on sentences with conjunctions

**The following sentences are run-on sentences. Rewrite them as complete sentences by adding the conjunctions *and, or, so,* or *but*.**

1. I am busy with work I am studying. _I am busy with work, or I am studying._

   _____

2. Almost everyone in her neighborhood speaks her language she does not have to use English. _____

   _____

3. Credit cards are convenient they are also dangerous. _____

   _____

4. I did not have experience I tried to get a job. _____

_____

5. Every time I travel, either I take a suitcase I take a backpack. _____

_____

6. My favorite flower is a rose my favorite color is red. _____

_____

## Language and Grammar Focus

### Dependent Clauses

A **dependent clause** is a clause that is not a complete sentence by itself. It has a subject and a verb, but it does not have a complete idea. A dependent clause often starts with a **subordinating conjunction** like *because, before, since, when, after,* or *while*. A dependent clause must always be attached to a main (or independent) clause to make one complete sentence. The dependent clause can come before or after the main clause without changing the meaning, but the punctuation is different.

| dependent clause | main clause |
|---|---|

**When I talk to my friend,** she likes to tell me about her adventures.

| main clause | dependent clause |
|---|---|

My friend likes to tell me about her adventures **when I talk to her.**

## Exercise 3 Identifying dependent and main clauses

**Underline and label the clauses. Write *M* above the main clause in each sentence. Write *D* above the dependent clause.**

1. When I was growing up, everything was less expensive.

2. I guess things have changed since I was younger.

3. I was sad when we left my country.

4. When I am older, I want to have a big house with a patio and a swimming pool.

5. After you understand the meaning of a word, you can use the word in sentences.

6. It is only dangerous when the roads are wet.

7. Because the tide went out, the jellyfish were stranded on the beach.

8. My country was invaded many times before we formed our current government.

## Exercise 4 Correcting run-on sentences with punctuation

**Read the sentences. If the sentence is correct, write *C*. If the sentence is incorrect, write *I* and add correct punctuation, using a comma, semicolon, or period. Check for proper capitalization.**

__I__ 1. I went to the store with my friend Rachel. ~~we~~ *We* bought milk.

_____ 2. We brought the groceries through the back door after we got back.

_____ 3. I noticed that there was a little dirt on the floor the DVD player was missing nothing else was gone.

_____ 4. We called the police after we realized there had been a robbery.

_____ 5. The police arrived immediately and inspected the whole apartment.

_____ 6. They took statements later that afternoon they found the robbers and Rachel's DVD player.

## Exercise 5 Editing a paragraph

**Read the paragraph and edit as necessary. There are five more run-on sentences.**

I am the middle child in my family, *but* I wish I were not sometimes. My brother and sisters have an easier life than I do. My older brother is very responsible he is like a third parent my sisters and I have to do what he tells us if our parents are not home. He also has more freedom than we do. He can go out on the weekends and stay out late we have to be at home by 10:00 p.m. While my brother has more freedom than I do, my sisters have an easier life. They are twins, they get a lot of attention from our parents. My parents don't often spend time with me they spend most of their time with my sisters. Because I am not the oldest, I do not have the same power as my brother, but I do not get the extra attention either. As a result, I wish I were the oldest or the youngest child rather than the middle child.

### In **Review** you will . . .

- review topics and controlling ideas.
- practice editing a paragraph for unity.
- practice identifying thesis statements.
- practice correcting run-on sentences.

In Putting It All Together you will review what you learned in this unit.

## Exercise 1 Identifying topics and controlling ideas

**Circle the topic and underline the controlling idea in the topic sentences below.**

1. Pizza is easy to make if you follow these steps.
2. If you compare an apartment with a house, you will find several important differences.
3. There are several ways to reduce stress.
4. Not getting enough sleep can have negative effects on a student.
5. One of my backpacking trips was almost my last.
6. A good journalist has to have special talents and skills.

## Exercise 2 Editing a paragraph

**Read the paragraph. Draw a line through the sentences that are irrelevant. There are five irrelevant sentences.**

When I want to eat steak, I go to my favorite restaurant, Saltgrass Steakhouse, because I always have a good experience. I love walking through the big, heavy, wooden doors because the spicy smell of grilled meat makes my mouth water. The hostess knows my family, and she always gives us a good seat where we can watch the other customers and enjoy the cowboy decorations on the walls. The service is friendly and efficient. On the other hand, the cook is often grumpy. He yells at the waiters sometimes. The waiters always bring crayons and paper for my daughters. I always order the rib-eye steak because the grilled meat is tender and seasoned with delicious spices. After dinner, we talk and enjoy the atmosphere. It is not good to eat there every day because the beef has a lot of fat. All red meat has a lot of fat, and it can cause problems such as high cholesterol. I like to eat at Saltgrass Steakhouse once a month, but I would eat there more often if I had the money. It has the best steak in the city.

**Read the short essay. The thesis statement is missing. Choose the best thesis statement from the list following the short essay.**

A good game that is simple and fun for everyone is hopping tag. Children love it because it is fun, and adults love it because there is no fancy equipment and anyone who can jump can participate.

---

Hopping tag follows the same basic procedure as regular tag with a few additional rules. First, decide on the boundaries. It is a good idea to play outside in a backyard or in a park because you will want to have plenty of room to move around. Once you have a good place to play, choose one person to be *It*. That person must then "tag" another player by bumping into the person. Then the tagged player becomes *It*. Finally, in hopping tag all players must keep their arms at their sides and their ankles together. This means that they must jump instead of run, and they must tag with their shoulders or hips rather than their hands. If a player does not keep his ankles together or his arms at his sides, he is cheating and must sit out for five minutes.

In conclusion, hopping tag is a great game for people of all ages because it requires no equipment and is easy to play. People usually have a good time because they look funny jumping around with their bodies straight and their arms at their sides. Most people spend a lot of time laughing when they play this game.

a. I often play hopping tag with my friends.

b. Hopping tag is easy to play if you follow the steps below.

c. Hopping tag is different from regular tag in two important ways.

## Exercise 4 Correcting run-on sentences with punctuation

Read the sentences. If the sentence is correct, write *C*. If the sentence is incorrect, write *I* and add correct punctuation, using a comma, semicolon, or period. Check for proper capitalization.

_____ 1. My father decided to go to dental school he was at the top of his class.

_____ 2. My writing has improved a great deal but I still need to work on my spelling and grammar.

_____ 3. When I am an industrial engineer I want to design kitchen appliances.

_____ 4. Administrative assistants play a very important role in an office; without them many businesses could not function.

_____ 5. I have never been afraid of snakes I think they are beautiful.

_____ 6. We lived in Malaysia after we got married.

## Exercise 5 Editing a paragraph

Read the paragraph and edit as necessary. There are six run-on sentences, and one mistake in punctuation between main clauses.

The memory of summer vacations at my grandmother's home in Ayutta, Thailand, always makes me happy. I loved this house very much because it was a beautiful and spacious place all the members of my family could gather together and enjoy nature. The house was located on a quiet stretch of river under a clear blue sky. It was a traditional, waterfront, Thai-style home it was built from teak wood. The tall, green trees around the house provided shade along the riverbank. Inside the house, there were many rooms my uncle's and my aunt's families could all come together at the same time. When we woke up, we could hear the sound of singing birds We children always rushed outside to breathe fresh air and dig our toes into the sand. In the afternoon, we played in the shade of the trees, swam in the river, and dug in the gardens. The adults watched us from the patio they could see us and we could see them. This home was the center place of my family I like to think about it when I feel lonely.

# UNIT 2 Descriptive Essays

## Unit Goals

### Rhetorical Focus

- descriptive organization

### Language and Grammar Focus

- prepositional phrases in descriptive writing
- details in sentences
- similes and simile structure
- adjectives in descriptive writing

Descriptive writing uses words to build images for the reader. These images may come from sights, sounds, smells, tastes, or even feelings. Good descriptive writing makes the reader feel as if he or she is present in the scene.

## Exercise 1 Thinking about the topic

**A. Discuss the picture with a partner.**

- Where do you think this place is?
- Imagine that you were in this place.
  What do you see around you?
  What do you hear?
  What do you smell?
- Imagine that you could taste one of the fruits. What does it taste like?
- Does this look like a place you would like to shop, or would you prefer to get your produce elsewhere?
- Describe some of the places people buy their fruits and vegetables.

**B. Make notes about a favorite place where you like to get a specific food. It could be a market, a tree near your house, a restaurant, or another place. Think about the sights, sounds, and feelings of the place. Then discuss in small groups.**

Sometimes one particular experience can create a memory that stays with us for many years. The following reading describes Esmeralda Santiago's memories of the guavas she ate as a child.

# How to Eat a Guava

There are guavas at the **Shop & Save.** I pick one the size of a tennis ball and finger the prickly stem end. It feels familiarly bumpy and firm. The guava is not quite ripe; the skin is still a dark green. I smell it and imagine a pale pink center, the seeds tightly embedded in the flesh.

A ripe guava is yellow although some varieties have a pink tinge. The skin is thick, firm, and sweet. Its heart is bright pink and almost solid with seeds. The most delicious part of the guava surrounds the tiny seeds. If you don't know how to eat a guava, the seeds end up in the **crevices** between your teeth.

When you bite into a ripe guava, your teeth must grip the bumpy surface and sink into the thick edible skin without hitting the center. It takes experience to do this, as it's quite tricky to determine how far beyond the skin the seeds begin.

Some years, when the rains have been **plentiful** and the nights cool, you can bite into a guava and not find many seeds. The guava bushes grow close to the ground, their branches **laden with** green then yellow fruit that seem to ripen overnight. These guavas are large and juicy, almost seedless, their roundness enticing you to have one more, just one more, because next year the rains may not come.

A green guava is sour and hard. You bite into it at its widest point, because it's easier to grasp with your teeth. You hear the skin, meat, and seeds crunching inside your head, while the inside of your mouth explodes in little spurts of sour.

You **grimace,** your eyes water, and your cheeks disappear as your lips purse into a tight O. But you have another and then another, enjoying the crunchy sounds, the acid taste, the gritty texture of the unripe center. At night, your mother makes you drink **castor oil,** which she says tastes better than a green guava. That's when you know for sure that you're a child and she has stopped being one.

I had my last guava the day we left Puerto Rico. It was large and juicy, almost red in the center, and so **fragrant** that I didn't want to eat it because I would lose the smell. All the way to the airport I scratched at it with my teeth, making little dents in the skin, chewing small pieces with my front teeth, so that I could feel the texture against my tongue, the tiny pink pellets of sweet.

Today, I stand before a stack of dark green guavas, each perfectly round and hard. The one in my hand is tempting. It smells faintly of late summer afternoons and **hopscotch** under the mango tree. But this is autumn in New York, and I'm no longer a child.

The guava joins its sisters under the harsh fluorescent lights of the **exotic** fruit display. I push my cart away, toward the apples and pears of my adulthood, their nearly seedless ripeness predictable and bittersweet.

Santiago, Esmeralda. "Prologue: How to Eat a Guava." *When I Was Puerto Rican.* New York: Vintage Books, 1993.

**Shop & Save:** a supermarket
**crevices:** narrow openings; gaps
**plentiful:** producing great quantities; abundant
**laden with:** heavily loaded or weighed down

**grimace:** show a facial expression of disgust or pain
**castor oil:** an oil used to help digestion
**fragrant:** having a pleasant smell
**hopscotch:** a children's hopping game
**exotic:** mysteriously foreign

## Exercise 3 Understanding the text

**Write *T* for true or *F* for false for each statement.**

_____ 1. The author is standing in a supermarket, eating fruit.

_____ 2. When it rains more and is cool at night, the fruit produce more seeds.

_____ 3. The author remembers only sweet guavas.

_____ 4. The last guava the author tasted was on the day she returned to Puerto Rico.

## Exercise 4 Responding to the text

**Respond to the reading by answering the following questions.**

1. Circle your favorite paragraph from the reading. What are some of the words or phrases that the author uses to describe the experience of eating a guava?

   _____

   _____

   _____

2. How do you think the author felt when she saw the guavas in the supermarket?

   _____

   _____

   _____

3. Reread the fifth and sixth paragraphs of the reading. Why do you think the author used to eat green guavas? Do you think she ate them alone or with friends? How do you think she felt afterwards?

   _____

   _____

   _____

4. What do you think the author means when she says, "the guava joins its sisters" in the last paragraph. Why do you think she uses the word *sister* for a fruit?

   _____

   _____

   _____

## Exercise 5 Freewriting

**Write for ten to fifteen minutes in your journal. Choose from topics below or an idea of your own. Express your thoughts and feelings. Don't worry about mistakes.**

- The author talks about her experiences of eating guavas as a child. What was your favorite food as a child?
- What is a food that you don't like? Why don't you like it?
- Write about a favorite drink or food. In what way is this drink or food healthy or unhealthy?
- Do all fruits and vegetables taste the same no matter where you buy them? Explain.

## In **Writing Process Step 2** you will . . .

- learn about descriptive organization.
- brainstorm ideas and specific vocabulary to use in your writing.
- determine the audience and purpose for your descriptive essay.
- create an outline for your essay.

**WRITING TASK** People have strong feelings about food. They associate food with important events and people in their lives. In this unit, you will write a descriptive essay about a food you feel strongly about—one you really like or dislike. Go to the Web to use the Online Writing Tutor.

## Exercise 1 Brainstorming ideas

Think of a food you really like or dislike. On a separate piece of paper, write down your ideas about this food in a word web like the one below. Think about the food's taste, smell, appearance, preparation, any sounds you associate with it, or the context in which you eat it.

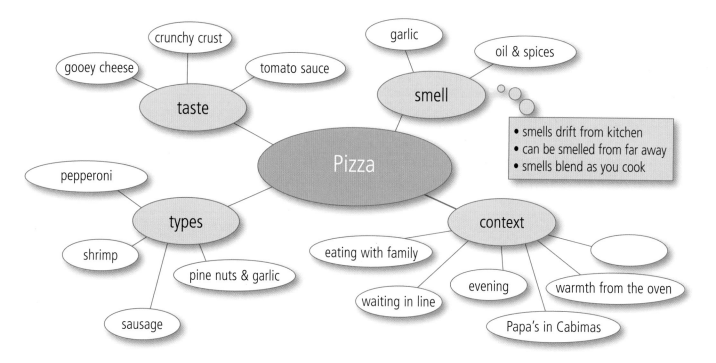

## Exercise 2 Identifying audience and purpose

Before you write, think about who will read your essay and what you want your readers to learn from the essay. Answer the following questions on a separate piece of paper.

1. Who will read your essay?
2. What type of relationship do you have with your readers?
3. What do you want your readers to learn from reading your essay?
4. What will your readers expect to read in your essay?

## Exercise 3 Brainstorming vocabulary

**A. Think about the food you want to write about. Add two more words to each set to describe the food. Then circle the words you would like to use.**

1. **Taste:** salty, sour, bitter, sweet, juicy, _____, _____

2. **Touch:** soft, hard, chewy, tough, crunchy, _____, _____

3. **Smell:** sweet, comforting, sharp, strong, faint, _____, _____

4. **Sight:** small, big, tempting, smooth, _____, _____

**B. Practice using these words in sentences. Use your dictionary for help.**

_____

_____

_____

_____

_____

_____

## Rhetorical Focus

### Descriptive Organization

In a **descriptive essay,** a writer uses details to tell how a subject looks, sounds, smells, tastes, or feels. The essay should make the reader feel like responding to what he or she is reading.

### Introduction
- The hook introduces the object or event in the description and gets the reader's attention.
- The middle sentences provide the background.
- The thesis statement tells why the object described is important to the writer.

### Body Paragraphs
- Most of the description is in the body paragraphs.
- Adjectives and adverbs make the experience more vivid.
- The scene is often described with prepositions and prepositional phrases that specify location or position in space.
- Comparisons, such as similes, can make the writing more descriptive, familiar, and expressive.

### Conclusion
- The conclusion gives the writer's final opinion about the item described.

Read the essay. According to the writer, where can you get the best pizza?

# The Best Pizza in Town and Maybe the World

I have suffered a great deal because of a terrible addiction to pizza. Basically, I enjoy pizza too much. In fact, I enjoy it so much that I won't share it, not even with my mother. People often think of pizza as junk food, but because you can put almost anything on a pizza, you can make it quite healthy if you want. People in my hometown of Cabimas, Venezuela, laugh at me and call me the Pizza King of Cabimas. Actually, it is a name that I am proud of. I have eaten pizza in many places, and none is as good as the pizza of Cabimas.

The best place to eat pizza in Cabimas is at Papa's. Customers have to wait in line to get a table, but the wait is worth it. Once they are seated, pizza-lovers can choose from many varieties of pizza, such as pizza with shrimp and smoked oysters or pizza with pine nuts and garlic, but my favorite is the sausage and pepperoni. First of all, it is big. When the waiter puts it down in front of me, I feel happy because I will get enough to eat. It smells of garlic, oil, and spices. And it looks delicious, too. The sauce oozes out from under a layer of rich melted cheese. The best part is the first bite. I sink my teeth into a slightly crunchy crust, thick tomato sauce, and gooey cheese, and I am in heaven. I can eat two of these pizzas in one night even though I know I will have a stomachache afterwards.

Now that I am in the United States, I am trying different kinds of pizzas here. I have never seen so many different pizza restaurants! I want to try them one by one. So far, some of them are delicious, but I am convinced that the best pizza in the world is still at Papa's restaurant, a couple of blocks from the house where I grew up.

## Exercise 5 Examining the student essay

**A. Examine the essay by responding to the questions and statements below.**

1. What is surprising in the writer's hook?

   _____

   _____

2. What is the main idea of the introduction?
   a. how the writer has suffered
   b. where to get the best pizza
   c. the writer's addictions
   d. the writer's hometown

3. How do the descriptive details help you understand what is special about Papa's pizza?

   _____

   _____

4. The conclusion ends with a(n)—
   a. description of the pizza served at Papa's.
   b. restatement of the main idea in the introduction.
   c. story about one visit to a pizza restaurant.
   d. invitation to eat pizza.

**B. Examine the writer's probable audience and purpose by selecting the correct answers below. Then compare your answers with a partner.**

1. The purpose of this essay is to—
   a. explain a past work experience.
   b. show how much the writer likes pizza.
   c. show the superiority of Papa's pizza.
2. Who might be most interested in this essay?
   a. an employer in Cabimas
   b. a tourist visiting Cabimas
   c. someone looking for a job in Cabimas

## Exercise 6 Completing an outline

To help you understand the organization of descriptive essays, use the essay about pizza to fill in the missing information in the outline below.

**Introduction**

**Topic:** _Pizza in Cabimas_____

**Hook:** _I'm addicted to pizza._____

**Background Information:** _don't share pizza with anyone, called the Pizza_

_King, tried pizza in many places_

**Thesis Statement:** 1. _____

**Body Paragraph**

**Details:** _places to eat pizza, Papa's, types of pizza_ 2. _____

_____

**Words or Phrases:** _gooey, cheesy, rich melted cheese, stomachache, big,_

_spices, crunchy crust_

**Conclusion**

**Final Opinion:** 3. _____

_____

## Exercise 7 Writing an outline

**GO ONLINE**

Throughout this book you will use outlining to help you plan the essays you will write. You can think of an outline like a map. It tells you where you are going with your thesis, and it organizes the ideas you will use to get your point across.

Writing your ideas on paper before you start to write a draft will help you organize and focus your essay. Also it will free you to develop each idea without being afraid that you will forget the idea that comes next.

On the Web you will find an outline template for Unit 2. Print it out and use it to plan your essay about a food you enjoy.

In **Writing Process Step 3** you will . . .

- learn about prepositional phrases.
- learn to use descriptive details in your writing.
- learn about similes in descriptive writing.
- write a first draft of your descriptive essay.

## Exercise 1 Reading a student essay

Read the essay. What main event does the writer describe?

# Food from the Sea

My father told me that we should always respect nature and learn where our food comes from. He said that food tastes better when you get it yourself and eat it in a natural place. To show me this was true, my father took me to the ocean, where we caught our own delicious crabs and ate them.

I will always remember the taste of the crabs we caught that day. The beach was quiet and still at six o'clock. The tide had just come in, so there were many crabs walking slowly on the white sand. We sat a few feet away from my father's special crab traps. The traps were made of bamboo, and they looked like round cages, but one side had a small entrance for the crab to go in. There were some small, fragrant fish in the trap. The fishy smell made the crabs hungry, so they crawled into the traps. We watched the crabs walk into the traps, and I smelled the strong smell of the dark, oily fish. Overhead, we heard the sounds of seagulls and pelicans in the sky. I think the seagulls wanted to eat the fish, too. Once the traps were full, we took off our shoes and threw them over our shoulders so we could walk on the wet sand and feel the water pushing and pulling at the beach. Later, we built a fire and ate boiled crabs on the beach. We cracked their shells. The meat was white and pinkish and tender. It tasted sweet and a little salty. We did not want to stop eating crab. We sat on the sand surrounded by crab shells and watched the sun go down into the ocean.

From that day on, I knew my father was right. Food tastes best when it is something that you have caught or grown yourself. I have eaten crab many times since then, but it has never tasted as good as it did that day.

## Exercise 2 Examining the student essay

**Examine the essay by answering the following questions.**

1. What does the place described in the essay look like?

   _____

   _____

2. How does the writer feel about the experience?

   _____

   _____

3. What sounds, sights, smells, or tastes are described?

   _____

   _____

4. What final opinion does the writer give in the conclusion?

   _____

   _____

## Language and Grammar Focus

### Prepositional Phrases in Descriptive Writing

A **prepositional phrase** is made up of a preposition + a noun phrase or pronoun.

| prepositional phrase | | prepositional phrase |
|---|---|---|

The boat slowly sank **with the water level** until it rested **on the bay floor**.

Prepositional phrases are important in descriptive writing. They show the position, location, or direction of objects in space and time. We can also use prepositional phrases to show manner or attitude.

Prepositional phrases show position and location.

> **On the right,** there were many kinds of cheeses arranged **in rows**.

Prepositional phrases show direction.

> We took the boat out **on the water**.

> The idea was to carry the food **across the street**.

Prepositional phrases show time.

> at six in the morning     in that sweet moment     on Thursday

Prepositional phrases show manner or feeling.

> We waited **in anticipation**.     He looked **with interest**.

## Exercise 3 Using prepositional phrases

**A. Complete the sentences below using a prepositional phrase to add more detail. Use the questions in parentheses to guide you.**

1. Yesterday _at 3 o'clock_ I took my sister to the new market near our house. (What time?)

2. We watched _____ as the seller arranged the fruit. (How did you feel?)

3. _____ rows of ripe fruit stretched out, as far as the eye could see. (In what direction?)

4. _____ fruit-sellers arranged fresh fish and shellfish. (Where?)

5. Some of the best bargains can be had _____ when sellers lower their prices to sell what won't keep until the next day. (When?)

6. Once we made our purchases, we headed _____ for a picnic in the warm sunshine. (Where?)

**B. Look back at the student essay on page 37. Underline the prepositional phrases. Compare your answers with a partner.**

---

## Language Focus 🔍

### Adding Details to Sentences

**Details** tell what something looks like, or how it sounds, feels, tastes, or smells. We can use nouns, adjectives, adverbs, and verbs to add details. The more specific the details are, the more effective and interesting the writing will be. Clear, specific details allow the reader to create a picture in his or her mind of what is being described. Compare the general sentences below with ones that have specific details.

| **General Sentences** | **Sentences with Specific Details** |
| --- | --- |
| The crabs were <u>good</u>. | The crabs were **tender and sweet with a salty taste**. |
| He bought some <u>fruit</u>. | He bought some **sweet, juicy strawberries**. |
| She <u>walked</u> to the door. | She **tiptoed** to the door. |
| She walked to the door. | She walked **quickly and silently** to the door. |

## Exercise 4 Adding specific details

Rewrite the general sentences below with more specific details.
Use adjectives, nouns, verbs, and adverbs.

| General | With Specific Details |
| --- | --- |
| 1. He bought a vegetable. | *He bought some bright green spinach.* |
| 2. We returned from the store. | |
| 3. I entered the room. | |
| 4. My friend cleaned the spinach. | |
| 5. We put the spinach in the pan. | |
| 6. Our guests enjoyed the dinner. | |

## Language and Grammar Focus

### Similes

Descriptive writing may use **similes** to make something seem more familiar or more creative. Similes make ideas easier to understand, and they can also express feelings. Similes are often used in literature and poetry. Look at the famous examples below:

*The sun was like a glowing ball of fire.*
   —Shakespeare

*I was young and easy . . . and happy as the grass was green.*
   —Dylan Thomas

*My love is like a red, red rose.*
   —Robert Burns

### Simile Structure

A simile can use the preposition like + noun or noun phrase.

The dog looked **like** a <u>mop</u>.
The stars lined the night sky **like** a <u>diamond necklace</u>.

A simile can also use as . . . as + noun or noun phrase. This kind of simile also uses an adjective.

He is **as** <u>clever</u> **as** a <u>fox</u>.
The girl's hair was **as** <u>wet</u> **as** <u>noodles in a bowl of soup</u>.

## Exercise 5 Understanding similes

**Reread the example similes on page 40. Then answer the following questions. Discuss your answers with a partner.**

1. How does Shakespeare's simile help you picture what the sun looked like?

   _____

   _____

2. Why would Thomas compare green grass to being young, easy, and happy?

   _____

   _____

3. Why does Burns compare love with a red rose? _____

   _____

## Exercise 6 Identifying similes

**Match the first half of each sentence with the second half.**

| | | |
|---|---|---|
| _f_ 1. The house | a. smelled sweet like honey. |
| ____ 2. The ocean | b. is as solid as a rock. |
| ____ 3. The cold wind | c. sparkles like a diamond. |
| ____ 4. Their friendship | d. was as fast as a bullet. |
| ____ 5. The train | e. cut sharply like a knife. |
| ____ 6. The air | f. was as huge as a castle. |

## Exercise 7 Writing similes

**Complete the sentences to make your own similes with *like* or *as*.**

1. The place where I grew up is _as hot as an oven._____

2. The cake is _____

3. My favorite music is _____

4. Coffee is _____

5. TV cooking shows are _____

## Exercise 8 Writing a first draft

GO ONLINE

Review your outline. Then write the first draft of a descriptive essay on a food you strongly like or dislike. Go to the Web to use the Online Writing Tutor.

## Exercise 9 Peer editing a first draft

A. After writing a first draft, it is helpful to get feedback on your ideas. Exchange essays with two other people. For each essay you read, answer the Peer Editor's Questions on a separate piece of paper. Then discuss your responses.

GO ONLINE

### Peer Editor's Questions

1. What is your favorite part of the essay?

2. Do you have any questions for the writer?

3. Why is the food important to the writer?

4. As you read, can you imagine how the food looks, feels, tastes, and smells?

5. Where does the essay need more details?

6. What is the writer's opinion of the food?

**Go to the Web to print out a peer editor's worksheet.**

B. Review your feedback and the organization guidelines on page 33. Make notes for your revision. In this step, you may add, remove, or rewrite information to clarify your ideas.

### In **Writing Process Step 4** you will . . .

- learn about the use and formation of adjectives.
- learn about adjective order.
- learn how to describe feelings.
- edit your first draft and write a final draft.

Now that you have written a first draft, it is time to edit. Editing involves making changes to your writing to improve it and to correct mistakes.

## Language and Grammar Focus

### Using Adjectives in Descriptive Writing

**Adjectives** are words that describe nouns: people, places, and things. Adjectives appear in different positions in the sentence.

Adjectives usually come after an article and before a noun.

We sat in the **roasting** sun.

Adjectives can also occur after some stative verbs such as *appear, be, become, feel, look,* or *seem.*

I was **hungry**.
He became **thoughtful**.

Use *and* to separate two adjectives that follow a verb.

He was **sick** and **tired**.

Separate more than two adjectives with commas and the word *and.*

We were **excited**, **nervous**, and **anxious**.

## Exercise 1 Identifying adjectives

Read the following sentences. Circle the adjectives and underline the nouns they describe.

1. The beach was quiet and still.
2. Many crabs were walking slowly on the white sand.
3. The traps looked like round cages.
4. There were some small, fragrant fish in the trap.
5. The fishy smell made the crabs hungry.
6. I smelled the strong smell of the dark, oily fish.
7. The meat was white, pinkish, and tender.
8. It tasted sweet.

GO ONLINE

## Language and Grammar Focus

### Formation of Adjectives

Adjectives may be formed from verbs. Many of these adjectives are formed by adding *-ing* to verbs.

entertain   entertain**ing**          excite   excit**ing**
*(an entertaining film)*              *(an exciting novel)*

The past participles of verbs can function as adjectives.

break   brok**en**                     excite   excit**ed**
*(a broken arm)*                      *(an excited child)*

Nouns may also function as adjectives when they are used to describe or modify other nouns. They are called noun modifiers.

A store that sells shoes ——→   a **shoe** store

## Exercise 2 Formation of adjectives

**Circle the adjective. Write the verb or noun form of the adjective in the blank at the end of the sentence.**

1. After lunch, we went to the (fruit) stand. _fruit_____

2. It was a frightening story. _____

3. Blending foods together can cause interesting flavors to emerge. _____

4. In the past, a refrigerator was sometimes called an ice box. _____

## Language and Grammar Focus

### Describing Feelings

Some adjectives ending in *-ed* and *-ing* can be used to talk about feelings and emotions; for example, *interesting, interested, boring, bored, confusing, confused.*

The adjectives ending in *-ed* (past participles) describe how people feel about something.

The **interested** students listened to the story. (= The students felt interest.)

The confused tourists did not know where to go. (= The tourists felt confusion.)

The adjectives ending in *-ing* describe the noun that causes the emotion or feeling.

The students heard an **interesting** story. (= The story caused interest.)

The movie had a **confusing** plot. (= The plot caused confusion.)

## Exercise 3 Describing feelings

**Circle the correct adjective in each sentence.**

1. The movie was very (bored / boring).
2. The audience was very (confused / confusing) by the story.
3. As a student, I found the class very (interested / interesting).
4. The speaker was very (excited / exciting) by the topic.
5. The children were (tired / tiring) by the game.

GO ONLINE

## Language and Grammar Focus

### Order of Adjectives
Adjectives appear in a particular order, according to their function.

| QUALITY / OPINION | SIZE | AGE | SHAPE | COLOR | ORIGIN | MATERIAL | PURPOSE / KIND |
|---|---|---|---|---|---|---|---|
| interesting boring | huge small | old new | round square | blue white | Mexican European | wooden iron | picnic wedding |

We put **huge** plates of **Mexican** food out on the **wooden picnic** table.

My mother had a **beautiful, small, antique, Tahitian pearl** necklace that she wore for special occasions.

Rosa and Pablo bought **gold wedding** rings.

## Exercise 4 Using adjectives in the correct order

**A. Write *C* if the adjectives are in the correct order. Write *I* if they are not.**

_C_ 1. The museum had a fantastic new sculpture outside.

_____ 2. They walked down the marble old giant staircase.

_____ 3. The restaurant had entrance wooden doors.

_____ 4. There were bright blue lights to mark the entrance.

_____ 5. There was a new small table in the corner.

**B. Add two adjectives for each of the sentences.**

1. It was a _fast_____, _____ car.

2. They lived in a _____, _____ house.

3. The house was located on a _____, _____ street.

4. She enjoyed the _____, _____ dinner.

## Exercise 5 Building vocabulary with adjectives

Circle a more specific adjective to replace the underlined word.

1. The food tasted good. (exquisite / obscure / uninteresting)

2. Good nutrition is important for a child's growth. (ephemeral / unimportant / fundamental)

3. The vegetables that had been stored too long were bad. (intense / brilliant / spoiled).

4. Farming is always a difficult industry; weather can easily ruin an entire year's crop. (undemanding / risky / frequent)

5. It is nice to see the innovations that have been made to the science of weather prediction. (unreliable / challenging / fascinating)

## Exercise 6 Editing a paragraph

Read the paragraph and edit as necessary. There are six more mistakes in adjective order.

Everyone in my family gathers for dinner every Saturday night, all my sisters and brothers and their children. It is an important family tradition. My husband and I leave at two in the afternoon, and take the ~~drive long~~ *long drive* to my parents' house. They live on a narrow dirt road. In summer we have to close the windows to the car so that the dust doesn't come in. My parents live in a large, wooden, white house, with a red, old, big door. There is a kitchen spacious where everyone helps prepare the dinner. The thing I love the most about the house is walking into the dining room after we finish preparing the dinner. The old, beautiful table is set with a lace white tablecloth and round, huge platters of food. Then everyone sits down in the big, comfortable chairs to enjoy the dinner. We talk and eat for hours and enjoy our family. Everyone feels happy, relaxed, and full. Late at night, we finally say goodbye until the next Saturday.

## Exercise 7 Editing your first draft and rewriting

Review your essay for mistakes. Use the checklist below. Then write a final draft.
Go to the Web to use the Online Writing Tutor.

GO ONLINE

# Editor's Checklist

**Put a check (✓) as appropriate.**

CONTENT AND ORGANIZATION

○ 1. Does your introduction include a hook to get your readers' attention?

○ 2. Do you provide background information?

○ 3. Do your body paragraphs provide enough details to help your readers picture, feel, taste, and smell the food you are describing?

○ 4. Did you use similes correctly to make your writing more descriptive?

○ 5. Does your conclusion clearly communicate your opinion of the food you describe?

LANGUAGE

○ 6. Did you use adjectives after articles and before nouns?

○ 7. Did you use adjectives immediately after stative verbs?

○ 8. If a sentence has more than one adjective, do the adjectives appear in the correct order?

○ 9. Did you use prepositional phrases to show location and time?

**Go to the Web to print out a peer editor's worksheet.**

In **Review** you will . . .

- review the use of prepositional phrases.
- practice using adjectives in descriptive writing.

**In Putting It All Together you will review what you learned in this unit.**

## Exercise 1 Identifying prepositional phrases

**Circle the prepositional phrases.**

1. On Saturday we walked to the pizza restaurant in Cabimas.
2. The pizzas that came out of the oven looked delicious.
3. We watched with excitement as the waiter brought the pizza to our table.
4. My favorite pizza comes with sausage and mushrooms on top.
5. The cheese on top of it is hot, and the crust crunches in your mouth when you bite it.
6. There are four chairs around each table.

## Exercise 2 Identifying adjectives

**Read the following sentences. Circle the adjectives and underline the nouns they describe.**

1. The table was long and narrow.
2. It had tall, straight chairs on each side.
3. It gave the dining room an elegant feeling.
4. Small candles decorated each table.
5. In front of each chair was a delicate lace napkin.
6. Each napkin sat on top of a shiny dinner plate.
7. The guests arrived in beautiful clothing and full of lively conversation.

## Exercise 3 Building vocabulary with adjectives

**Rewrite each sentence by choosing the correct synonym for the underlined adjective from the words in parentheses.**

1. The big jungle was filled with life. (vast / wild / exciting)

   _____

   _____

2. The old temples could be seen for miles. (ancient / stone / huge)

   _____

   _____

3. The small steps led to a tower. (gray / soaring / narrow)

   _____

   _____

4. A <u>wide</u> view could be seen from the top of the mountain. (spectacular / panoramic / green)

_____

_____

5. People marveled at the <u>jungle</u> landscape. (mesmerizing / ageless / tropical)

_____

_____

6. The company produced a/n <u>interesting</u> new music application. (unusual / boring / loud)

_____

_____

## Exercise 4 Using adjectives in the correct order

**Write *C* if the adjectives are in the correct order. Write *I* if they are not.**

_____ 1. The thing I like most about visiting my parents is sleeping in my bed old.

_____ 2. Katerina's baby was small and beautiful.

_____ 3. Sebastian enjoyed the delicious meal gourmet.

_____ 4. They painted the house an antique lovely gray.

_____ 5. There were 14 people seated in the old dining room.

_____ 6. Montreal is a city with a history rich.

### In Timed Writing you will . . .

• practice writing with a time limit.

Practice your test-taking skills with the following practice topic. Read the prompt. Then follow the steps below.

> Describe a place that has special significance for you. Describe where it is, what the place looks like, the people who live there, and the feelings you have about the place.

### Step 1 **BRAINSTORMING:** 5 minutes

Write down ideas and vocabulary for your essay on a separate piece of paper. Use a word web like the one on page 32 to collect ideas. Include details about the sounds, sights, and people that relate to the place you are writing about. Also, consider feelings and memories of events that happened there.

### Step 2 **OUTLINING:** 5 minutes

Write an outline for your essay. Use another piece of paper if necessary.

| Introduction (First Paragraph) | |
| --- | --- |
| **Hook**<br>Get the reader interested. | |
| **Background Information**<br>Explain who, what, when, and where. | |
| **Thesis Statement**<br>Prepare for the description by focusing on the topic and what you will say about it. | |
| **Body Paragraphs (Middle Paragraphs)** | |
| **Topic Sentences**<br>Provide a controlling idea in each paragraph. | |
| **Descriptive Details**<br>Develop your controlling ideas. | |
| **Conclusion (Last Paragraph)** | |
| **Final Opinion**<br>Give your final opinion of the topic. | |

## Step 3   **WRITING:** 40 minutes

Use your brainstorming notes and outline to write your essay on a separate piece of paper.

## Step 4   **EDITING:** 10 minutes

When you have finished your essay, check it for mistakes using the checklist below.

**GO ONLINE**

### Editor's Checklist

**Put a check (✓) as appropriate.**

○ 1. Does the introduction include a hook and a thesis statement?

○ 2. Do the body paragraphs contain enough descriptive details? Do the details support the topic sentence of each body paragraph?

○ 3. Does the conclusion state a final opinion?

○ 4. Is the purpose of the essay clear?

○ 5. Did you use prepositional phrases to show location and time?

○ 6. Did you use similes to support your descriptions?

○ 7. Did you use the correct form and order of adjectives?

**Go to the Web to print out a peer editor's worksheet.**

**Test-Taking Tip**

When you finish your essay, read each paragraph sentence by sentence. Make sure every sentence is related to the topic sentence and to the sentence that came before it.

**Write a descriptive essay on one of the following topics.**

**Architecture:** Describe a famous building or structure. Where is it? Who built it? When? What is it used for? What do you like or dislike about it?

**Information Technology (IT):** Describe an important invention or development in information technology. What is the invention? How did it change the way people do things? Why do you think it is important?

**Medicine:** Describe an important innovation in medicine in the last 20 years. Who or what was responsible for this innovation? Why is this innovation important? How has this innovation changed medical professionals' and patients' lives?

**Sociology/Anthropology:** Describe a different culture or civilization. Why is it interesting to you? What could people learn from studying or visiting the people of this culture?

**Tourism:** Describe a tourist destination that you think is especially beautiful, historic, or significant. What is remarkable about it? Where is it? How do you get there? Describe the experience people have when they visit this place. Why do you think people should visit it?

# UNIT 3 Narrative Essays

## Unit Goals

### Rhetorical Focus

- narrative organization

### Language and Grammar Focus

- sequence in narrative essays
- subordinating conjunctions
- details in essays
- the past continuous in narrative essays
- past time clauses
- simultaneous activities

In psychology, formative experiences are experiences that shape how we see the world and what type of person we become later in life. In this unit, you will write a narrative about one such experience.

## Exercise 1 Thinking about the topic

A. Discuss the picture with a partner.

- What is happening in the picture?
- How do you think the person feels before, during, and after this experience?

B. Make notes about three important events or experiences in your life. Then discuss in small groups.

- Describe each event.
- Why was it important?
- How did it change you?

U.S. President and humanitarian Jimmy Carter wrote the following narrative passage. It describes his childhood experience "mopping cotton" on his father's farm during the 1930s. To kill insects that ate cotton plants, Carter's family covered each cotton plant with molasses mixed with poison.

# Breaking Ground to Be a Man

Mopping cotton was a terrible job. The **molasses** attracted **swarms** of flies and honeybees. They covered the buckets and followed us through the field. I usually wore short pants and a shirt during the warm months, but for this job I preferred to protect my legs with long pants. My pants quickly became covered with the poison, and stuck uncomfortably to my legs. In fact, everything about me was sticky. With time, my pants dried, and the sweet, sticky poison turned to hard sugar, so that at night my pants wouldn't fold but stood up alone in a corner or against the furniture. Covered with poison, they had to be washed separately from the other clothing, so we didn't change them every day. It was particularly disgusting to put them back on in the mornings.

Child farm worker, 1930s.

Adapted from Carter, James. *An Hour Before Daylight*. New York: Simon & Schuster, 2001. 180–181.

**molasses:** a thick, sugary syrup
**swarms:** large groups that are in motion (usually insects)

## Exercise 3 Understanding the text

**Write *T* for true or *F* for false for each statement.**

_____ 1. Carter wore shorts when he mopped cotton.

_____ 2. The poison turned from a liquid to a solid on his pants.

_____ 3. Carter folded his pants every night before he went to sleep.

_____ 4. Carter washed his pants with his other clothes.

## Exercise 4 Responding to the text

**Respond to the reading by answering the following questions.**

1. What three words would you use to describe Carter's experience?

   _____

2. How do you think the experience affected Carter's personality?

   _____

   _____

3. Is hard work good for children? Why or why not?

   _____

4. What is the most interesting sentence in the passage? Why is it interesting?

   _____

   _____

## Exercise 5 Freewriting

**Write for ten to fifteen minutes in your journal. Choose from topics below or an idea of your own. Express your thoughts and feelings. Don't worry about mistakes.**

- What do you remember most about your childhood summers?
- What jobs did you do to help your family when you were young?
- Write about a bad experience you have had with an insect or insects.
- Have you ever tried to grow something? What was the experience like?
- Tell a story from your life that supports the saying, "Experience is the best teacher."

### In **Writing Process Step 2** you will . . .

- learn about narrative organization.
- brainstorm ideas and specific vocabulary to use in your writing.
- determine the audience and purpose for your narrative essay.
- create an outline for your essay.

**WRITING TASK** Some experiences change our lives and form our personalities. In this unit, you will write a narrative essay about an experience that changed you or taught you something important. Go to the Web to use the Online Writing Tutor.

## Exercise 1 Brainstorming ideas

A. Think back to the events you wrote about and discussed in Exercise 1B on page 54. Can you add any more events to the list? Choose one of the events for your assignment. Fill in the chart with notes about the event.

| Event | What I Thought Before | What I Thought After |
|-------|-----------------------|----------------------|
|       |                       |                      |
|       |                       |                      |
|       |                       |                      |

B. On a separate piece of paper, brainstorm a list of details related to the event.

- When did it happen?
- Who were you with?
- Where did it happen?
- What happened first? Next? Last?

## Exercise 2 Identifying audience and purpose

A. Match the likely purpose to the audience.

| Audience | Purpose |
|----------|---------|
| 1. _____ friends | a. to show what I have learned |
| 2. _____ younger relatives | b. to show my ability to do a job |
| 3. _____ instructors | c. to teach by example |
| 4. _____ employers | d. to entertain |

B. On a separate piece of paper, write about a possible audience for your essay.

- Who will read your essay?
- What do they already know about you and your experience?
- Is your relationship with your readers formal or informal?
- What do they expect?
- How will your choice of audience and purpose affect the way you write your essay?

A. **Think about the event. Try to recall your actions and emotions. Add two or three more words to each set.**

1. **Actions:** hurry (to), gaze (at), warn (someone), suffer (from), notice (someone / something), _____, _____, _____

2. **Emotions:** nervous, eager, relieved, worried, amazed, confused, _____,

   _____, _____

B. **Circle words you would like to use from the sets. Practice using these words in sentences. Use your dictionary for help.**

_____

_____

_____

_____

_____

_____

## Rhetorical Focus

### Narrative Organization

A **narrative** is a story. It has an introduction that engages the reader's interest, details about the main event or action in the story, and a conclusion that describes the outcome.

**Introduction**

- The hook gets the reader's attention.
- The middle sentences introduce an event (the action of the story) by providing background information about the people, the place, and the time.
- The thesis statement prepares the reader for the action that follows.

**Body Paragraphs**

- The body paragraphs describe what happened in the story.
- They include details that bring the story to life.
- They often use time order to explain the event.

**Conclusion**

- A conclusion describes the outcome of the event.
- Narrative essays often end with a comment about the event's importance in the writer's life.

Read the essay. What was the writer's embarrassing incident?

## An Embarrassing Incident

Where I grew up, the rules for family life are very strict. My parents taught me that I should respect grandparents more than anyone else because grandparents had lived the longest. They had more knowledge about life, and no matter what they said, even if it did not make sense, they were right. Hugging or kissing grandparents was disrespectful. Instead, I was told to greet them by kissing their hand. I thought that everyone lived and thought just as I did. I soon found out this is not true.

One day, an American friend invited me to her birthday dinner. I was excited but at the same time nervous. I wanted her family to like me, and I wanted to use my best manners. Slowly, I walked up to the house and rang the bell. My friend came running out with a big smile, telling me she was happy that I came. Then she let me in and introduced me to her parents. They smiled and said hello. Later my friend said, "Come here. I want you to meet my grandpa." I followed her into the living room where her grandfather was sitting. She introduced us, and he reached out his hand. He was going to shake hands, but I thought he expected me to kiss his hand, so I did. He pulled his hand away and looked at me in a strange way. Everyone else in the room looked at me, and my friend started laughing.

I was confused. I sat down and tried to figure out what had happened. Just then, a little boy ran to my friend's grandfather and jumped on his lap. The little boy started to hug and kiss the grandfather. When I saw this, I got up, grabbed the little boy, and said, "NO." I guess I said it loudly because the room became silent, and all eyes were on me.

The next day at school my friend asked me why I kissed her grandfather's hand and why I told the little boy to get away from his grandfather. I explained my customs to her, and she explained hers to me. I learned that good manners are not the same in different countries. Fortunately, my friend and I stayed very good friends.

## Exercise 5 Examining the student essay

**A. Respond to the essay by answering the following questions.**

1. Why is the background information in the introduction important?

   _____

   _____

2. Why was the writer embarrassed?

   _____

   _____

3. What did the writer learn?

   _____

   _____

   _____

**B. Examine the organization of the essay by responding to the questions and statements below. Compare your answers with a partner.**

1. Underline the hook. Is it one sentence or two? _____

2. Circle the questions below that are answered in the background information.

   who?          what?          when?          which?

   where?        how?           why?

3. Underline the thesis statement. Is it one sentence or two? _____

4. Reread the body paragraphs. Circle one or two details or words that you like.

5. Reread the conclusion. Underline the sentences that explain what the writer learned. Was it a positive lesson or a negative lesson? _____

6. What audience would be most appropriate for this essay?
   a. the writer's friend in the story          b. a world cultures instructor

## Exercise 6 Writing an outline

**GO ONLINE**

Review your brainstorming ideas and your freewriting exercise. Then go to the Web to print out an outline template for your essay.

### In Writing Process Step 3 you will . . .

- learn about showing sequence in a narrative essay.
- learn to use subordinating conjunctions.
- learn about adding details to your essay.
- write a first draft of your narrative essay.

## Exercise 1 Reading a student essay

Read the essay. What is the scary secret?

### A Scary Secret

My sister and I made a dangerous mistake one summer. I was thirteen and my sister was fourteen. Our parents had taken us to the city where they grew up. We felt very grown up as we rode to the hotel in a taxi. The hotel was very big, and it had a blue tile floor. After we unpacked our suitcases, our parents wanted to go to the market. My mother told us not to go outside. "We won't," my sister promised, but I knew that she was lying. We had already decided to go out and explore this strange and beautiful city by ourselves.

As soon as my parents were out of sight, we got our things and went downstairs. We walked out of the hotel doors and down a narrow street. The sun was setting, and the light was very beautiful. We could hear the noises of traffic nearby, but the little street was quiet. Suddenly, a man with a gun stepped out from a doorway. He said, "Don't move!" He was short, and he was wearing a dark green jacket and sunglasses. He came very close, and we could smell cigarettes and something terrible in his breath. We were terrified and couldn't say anything. He said, "Give me your shoes." So I did. Then he took my sister's purse and her gold ring and ran away.

The horrible man was gone, but we were still afraid. I remember that I fell against my sister. I heard her take a deep breath; she was shaking. We ran back to the hotel, across the blue tile floor, and up to our room. We did not feel safe until we got into our room and locked the door behind us.

The man scared us, but he also taught us something important. Before this experience, we did not always listen to our parents. We now learned that we should obey them. My sister and I became obedient daughters, and we enjoyed the rest of our vacation. However, we decided not to tell our parents about our adventure. We knew they would punish us even though we had learned our lesson. This dangerous adventure is still a secret that I share with my sister.

## Exercise 2 Examining the student essay

**Examine the essay by responding to the following questions and statements.**

1. Underline and label the hook in the introduction. How does it get your attention?

_____

_____

2. Underline and label the thesis statement. What can you predict after reading the thesis?

_____

_____

3. This writer goes into great detail during one important moment in the story. Highlight the moment. Why does it make the story more powerful?

_____

_____

4. Why did the writer start a new body paragraph after writing that the man ran away?

_____

_____

5. The conclusion tells one thing the writer learned. What else do you think the writer learned?

_____

_____

## Language and Grammar Focus

### Showing Sequence in Narrative Essays

In narrative essays, we use **time expressions** to clarify the sequence of events.

We use connectors (**time adverbs**) such as *then, finally,* or *eventually* to link sentences within a paragraph.

We use **subordinating conjunctions** to link clauses within a sentence.

#### Time Adverbs

We use time adverbs such as *afterward, after that, eventually, finally, later, later on, now, then,* and *suddenly* as connectors. These connectors usually appear at the beginning of a sentence. When they do, they are immediately followed by a comma.

> *Then* is an exception. It is not followed by a comma.
>
> Our train was running late. **Finally,** it arrived.
>
> We got on board the train. **Then** we realized that we did not have money for the fare.

## Exercise 3 Identifying time adverbs

Reread the student essay on pages 61–62. List the time adverbs. On a separate piece of paper, write sentences of your own using the adverbs you found. After you finish, compare your sentences with a partner.

_____     _____

_____     _____

_____     _____

_____     _____

_____     _____

## Language and Grammar Focus

GO ONLINE

### Using Subordinating Conjunctions with the Simple Past

We use **subordinating conjunctions** such as *before, as soon as, after, when,* and *while* in complex sentences as connectors. Complex sentences contain a main (independent) clause and a dependent clause.

The main clause expresses the principal and independent idea of the sentence. The dependent clause expresses additional information about the main idea (for example, where or when it happened) but would be meaningless without the main idea.

Dependent time clauses tell us when something happened.

Subordinating conjunctions establish the time relationship between the dependent time clause and the main clause in the sentence. The subordinating conjunction starts the dependent clause, but the clauses can come in either order. We use a comma when the time clause comes before the main clause.

| time clause | main clause |
| --- | --- |
| **After** our parents left the hotel,<br>Before my **brother** was born, | we went into the street.<br>I was an only child. |

| main clause | time clause |
| --- | --- |
| We went into the street<br>I was an only child | **after** our parents left the hotel.<br>before my **brother** was born. |

## Exercise 4 Using subordinating conjunctions

**Combine each pair of sentences into one complex sentence. Use the subordinating conjunctions in parentheses to clarify time relationships.**

1. People harvested the apples. They stored them in cellars. (after)  _After people harvested the apples, they stored them in cellars._

2. People waited a long time for mail. It arrived. (before) _____

   _____

3. They saved enough money. They took a great vacation. (as soon as) _____

   _____

4. She thought carefully about which gift to buy. She bought the more expensive one. (before) _____

   _____

5. She paid for my college. She retired. (after) _____

   _____

6. He went straight to his lab. He got up in the morning. (as soon as) _____

   _____

## Language and Grammar Focus 🔍

### Adding Details to Essays

**Details** are facts, examples, illustrations, definitions, and descriptions. They answer *who, what, why, where, when,* and *how* questions. We add details to make our writing clearer and more effective.

| GENERAL | DETAIL | |
|---|---|---|
| | *Why?* | He was completely exhausted. |
| | *How?* | He traveled first class in an airplane. |
| He went on vacation. | *Where?* | He traveled to Africa. |
| | *Who?* | Although he traveled alone, he met many interesting people. |

## Exercise 5 Asking detail questions about an outline

Look at this outline and help the writer generate details by writing questions using *who, what, where, why,* or *how.*

---

**The Day I Became a Hero**

**Hook:** When I was eleven, I learned an important lesson about myself in gym class.

1. Questions: *What exactly did you learn? Where did you learn it?*
   *Who were you with? How did you learn it?*

**Thesis statement:** All the girls were afraid to jump over the pommel horse, but I was tired of waiting, so I decided to try.

2. Questions: _____

   _____

**Topic sentence:** I decided I wanted to go first.

3. Questions: _____

   _____

**Supporting detail:** I was overjoyed. I had jumped over the pommel horse without falling down.

4. Questions: _____

   _____

**Conclusion:** That day, I learned that I like to do things that are a little bit hard.

5. Questions: _____

   _____

## Exercise 6 Adding details to your outline

Give the outline for your essay to a partner and have him or her write questions about it for you.

## Exercise 7 Writing a first draft

GO ONLINE

Review your outline. Look at your partner's questions about your outline. Then write the first draft of a narrative essay about a learning experience that changed you or taught you something valuable. Go to the Web to use the Online Writing Tutor.

## Exercise 8 Peer editing a first draft

A. After writing a first draft, it is helpful to get feedback on your ideas. Exchange essays with two other people. For each essay you read, answer the Peer Editor's Questions on a separate piece of paper. Then discuss your responses.

GO ONLINE

### Peer Editor's Questions

1. What is your favorite part of the essay?

2. Are there any *who, what, where,* or *when* questions that you would like the writer to answer in the background?

3. What is the most important moment in the story? How did it make you feel?

4. What parts of the essay could be supported with more specific details?

5. What parts of the story seemed to have more detail than necessary?

6. What lesson did you learn? Is it the same as or different from the writer's lesson?

**Go to the Web to print out a peer editor's worksheet.**

B. Review your feedback and the organization guidelines on page 58. Make notes for your revision. In this step, you may add, remove, or rewrite information to clarify your ideas.

### In **Writing Process Step 4** you will . . .

- review the past continuous and learn about past time clauses.
- edit your first draft and write a second draft.

Now that you have written a first draft, it is time to edit. Editing involves making changes to your writing to improve it and to correct mistakes.

## Language and Grammar Focus

GO ONLINE

### Using the Past Continuous in Narrative Essays

In a narrative, you often need to describe actions in progress or to describe background actions.

To form the **past continuous,** use *was/were* and the base form of the verb + *-ing*.

Use the past continuous to talk about activities that were in progress at a specific time in the past. The activities began before the specific time and may also have continued after that time.

> At three o'clock we **were walking** home from school. My friend was **riding** his bicycle.

Also use the past continuous to describe background actions.

> The sun **was going** down, and the children **were** still **playing** on the grass.

> **!** We don't usually use stative verbs (*be, know, own, mean, seem, understand, love, believe, etc.*) in the past continuous. We use the simple past instead.
>
> I **didn't know** John then.
>
> **X** I wasn't knowing John then. (INCORRECT)

| AFFIRMATIVE STATEMENTS | | |
|---|---|---|
| **SUBJECT** | *WAS/WERE* | **VERB + *-ING*** |
| I | **was** | **working.** |
| They | **were** | |
| The sun | **was** | **shining.** |

| NEGATIVE STATEMENTS | | |
|---|---|---|
| **SUBJECT** | *WAS/WERE* + NOT | **VERB + *-ING*** |
| She | **wasn't** | **working.** |
| We | **weren't** | |
| The phone | **wasn't** | **ringing.** |

## Exercise 1 Identifying background action

Read the paragraph below and underline all the verbs that describe background actions.

# My Wedding

I will always remember my wedding day. It was beautiful. I woke up and looked outside. The sun <u>was shining</u>, and the birds were singing. It was as if they were talking to me, telling me to get up. In reality, the radio was playing and my brothers were arguing in the hallway, but it still felt romantic. My dress was hanging on the closet door. My mother was cooking breakfast in the kitchen, and the coffee was brewing. My father was talking on the phone to his brother, and they were discussing who was the better chess player. This was a constant argument between the two of them, but I knew my father was just trying to distract himself because he was feeling nervous.

## Exercise 2 Using the past continuous to describe actions in progress

Complete the following texts using the past continuous.

1. I wasn't home yesterday afternoon, <u>I was walking in the park.</u>

   _____

2. The president was satisfied. People _____

   _____

3. The ship captain was worried. A storm was coming, and _____

   _____

   _____

4. Thirty years ago, _____

   _____

5. During holidays, people _____

   _____

## Exercise 3 Setting the scene with background details

**Continue the stories below. Give background actions using the past continuous to help set the scene. Use the sample paragraph in Exercise 1 as a model.**

1. It was an ordinary day at school. _____
   _____
   _____
   _____
   _____
   _____
   _____
   _____
   _____
   _____
   _____
   _____
   _____.

2. It was a cold and rainy night. _____
   _____
   _____
   _____
   _____
   _____
   _____
   _____
   _____
   _____
   _____
   _____
   _____.

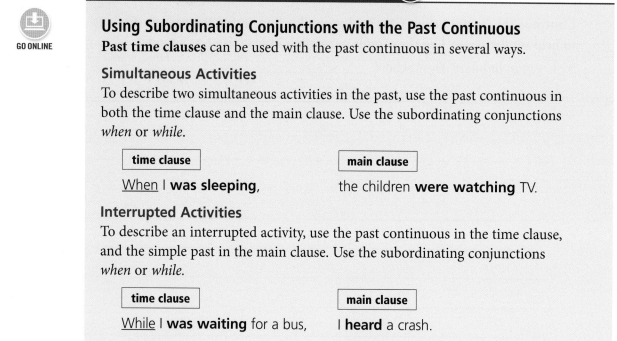

## Using Subordinating Conjunctions with the Past Continuous

**Past time clauses** can be used with the past continuous in several ways.

### Simultaneous Activities

To describe two simultaneous activities in the past, use the past continuous in both the time clause and the main clause. Use the subordinating conjunctions *when* or *while*.

| time clause | main clause |

When I **was sleeping**,          the children **were watching** TV.

### Interrupted Activities

To describe an interrupted activity, use the past continuous in the time clause, and the simple past in the main clause. Use the subordinating conjunctions *when* or *while*.

| time clause | main clause |

While I **was waiting** for a bus,          I **heard** a crash.

| main clause | time clause |

He **saw** the race          when he **was living** in Paris.

## Exercise 4 Identifying time clauses with the Past Continuous

Read the following sentences. Write *S* (simultaneous) if the sentence involves two simultaneous actions. Write *I* (interrupted) if the sentence involves one action interrupting another.

___S___ 1. Our company was developing new products while other companies were focusing on advertising.

_____ 2. We learned to read while we were living in Argentina.

_____ 3. The nurse was checking her blood pressure while the doctor was listening to her lungs.

_____ 4. The manager was flying while her employee was negotiating the deal.

_____ 5. Aaron called Mansoor while Mansoor was still driving.

_____ 6. The prime minister was sleeping when he received the call.

## Exercise 5 Using subordinating conjunctions

**Complete the sentences to create simultaneous or interrupted activities. Use *while* or *when* and the past continuous or the simple past.**

1. We were driving down the road _when a deer ran out in front of the car._

   _____

2. My parents were traveling in Indonesia _____

   _____

3. The professor was correcting papers _____

   _____

4. Ken was working on the electrical system _____

   _____

## Exercise 6 Editing a paragraph

**Read the paragraph and edit as necessary. There are seven more mistakes.**

# My Vacation in the Mountains

A few years ago my family went to the mountains to enjoy the beautiful views. In pictures, the mountains were always beautiful. The flowers were blooming, the sun was shining, and the people were smiling; however, our trip to the mountains was a disaster. While we traveled *were traveling* to our destination, the sun disappeared. It was rain. We were stay in a friend's small apartment. Every morning my father checked the sky. Every day it was the same: rainy and cloudy. One day, while my father was look at the clouds, a little sun began to shine through. My father saw the sun as soon as, we were jumping in the car. We drove to Jungfrau Mountain so we could take the tram to the top and enjoy the view. We eagerly got on the tram. It began to climb to the top of the mountain. However, while the tram was climbing, it becoming cloudy. When the tram arrived at the top of the mountain, we were in the middle of a cloud. We could not see anything. Our last day we went to the airport. While the plane taking off, the sun was beginning to shine again.

Review your essay for mistakes. Use the checklist below. Then write a final draft. Go to the Web to use the Online Writing Tutor.

GO ONLINE

## Editor's Checklist

**Put a check (✓) as appropriate.**

CONTENT AND ORGANIZATION

○ 1. Does a thesis statement with the main idea appear at the bottom of your first paragraph?

○ 2. Does each body paragraph have a clear topic sentence and specific supporting details?

○ 3. Do time expressions support the coherence of your essay?

○ 4. Does your conclusion explain the outcome and what you learned?

LANGUAGE

○ 5. Did you use the correct verb form to indicate sequence and interrupted or simultaneous actions?

○ 6. Did you check that stative verbs were used in the past simple?

○ 7. Do time adverbs and subordinating conjunctions help the flow of sentences?

**Go to the Web to print out a peer editor's worksheet.**

## In Review you will . . .

- review time adverbs and subordinating conjunctions.
- review the simple past and the past continuous.

In Putting It All Together you will review what you learned in this unit.

## Exercise 1 Using subordinating conjunctions

Rewrite the sentence(s) as either one or two correctly punctuated sentences. Use the words in parentheses.

1. Graduation day was very busy we went to the auditorium for the ceremony we came home and prepared the food for the celebration dinner. (after)

   _____

   _____

2. The chef went to the store to buy all the ingredients she came to the restaurant. (before)

   _____

   _____

3. I was learning to ride a bike I had a lot of bruises and cuts on my legs. (while)

   _____

   _____

4. Writing became easier for him he started doing it more frequently. (after)

   _____

   _____

5. I was in grade school I used to think I would never learn to play tennis. (when)

   _____

   _____

6. I never enjoyed eating vegetables I was young later on, I started to like the taste. (when)

   _____

   _____

7. My brother was living at home he taught me math. (while)

   _____

   _____

8. I was afraid of the water we moved to a house near a lake. (before)

_____

_____

9. My parents were visiting Paris they bought a beautiful ring. (while)

_____

_____

10. The cowboys were taking the cows to the trains. They sang to the animals to keep them calm. (while)

_____

_____

## Exercise 2 Reviewing the simple past and past continuous

**Write the correct form of the verbs in parentheses.**

Last Saturday was an exciting day for me. It was my birthday. I

worked until eight o'clock as usual. As I _____ (walk)
                                                    1.

to the bus stop, I _____ (look) for my younger brother.
                            2.

But that day he wasn't there. I _____ (think) it was
                                          3.

strange, but I _____ (imagine) he was out. When I
                        4.

_____ (arrive) at my house, I _____
        5.                                          6.

(notice) all the lights were turned off. While I _____
                                                          7.

(look for) my front door keys, I _____ (hear) a noise and
                                          8.

suddenly all the lights came on. All my family members were in my

house. When I opened the door, they all yelled, "Surprise!" It was a

surprise celebration for me, and I never suspected a thing!

## Exercise 3 Editing a paragraph

**Read the paragraph and edit as necessary. There are six mistakes in verb forms.**

### Strangers on a Bus

One morning I was wait at the bus stop. I was worried about being late for school, and I was anxiously waiting for the bus to arrive. It was late as usual, and I began to think of what I would tell my teacher. There were several people at the bus stop, and some of them were complaining. When the bus finally came, we all pushed our way on board. Someone folded his umbrella and sprayed water on me. I was felt upset, but fortunately, I got a place next to the window. I had a good view of the sidewalk. People was hurrying along clutching their umbrellas. Then a boy on a bike caught my attention. He was riding beside the bus and wave his arms. I heard passengers behind me shouting to the bus driver, but he refused to stop until we reached the next bus stop. Still, the boy kept riding. He was carried something over his shoulder and shouting. Finally, when we came to the next stop, the boy was running up to the door. I heard an excited conversation. Then the bus driver stood up and announced, "Did anyone lose a briefcase at the last stop?" A woman at the back of the bus shouted, "Oh my! It's mine." She pushed her way to the front and gratefully took the briefcase. She thanked the little boy with enthusiasm. After that, everyone on the bus began talking about what the boy had done, and the crowd of strangers suddenly became friendly.

### In **Timed Writing** you will . . .

• practice writing with a time limit.

Practice your test-taking skills with the following practice topic. Read the prompt. Then follow the steps below.

> Write a narrative essay about a time when you changed your mind about something. What prompted you to change your mind?

### Step 1   **BRAINSTORMING:** 5 minutes

Write down ideas and vocabulary for your essay on a separate piece of paper. You may want to use the chart on page 57. Remember to include specific details about the experience.

### Step 2   **OUTLINING:** 5 minutes

Write an outline for your essay. Use another piece of paper if necessary.

| Introduction (First Paragraph) | |
| --- | --- |
| **Hook**<br>Get the reader interested. | |
| **Background Information**<br>Tell who, when, and where. | |
| **Thesis Statement**<br>Prepare the reader for the story by focusing on the topic and what you will say about it. | |
| **Body Paragraphs (Middle Paragraphs)** | |
| **Topic and Controlling Idea**<br>List story details. What happened first?<br>What happened next? | |
| **Topic and Controlling Idea**<br>What happened last? How did the story end?<br>How did you or others feel? | |
| **Conclusion (Last Paragraph)** | |
| **Story's Importance**<br>What did you learn? | |

**Step 3** **WRITING:** 40 minutes

Use your brainstorming notes and outline to write your essay on a separate piece of paper.

**Step 4** **EDITING:** 10 minutes

When you have finished your essay, check it for mistakes using this checklist.

GO ONLINE

## Editor's Checklist

**Put a check (✓) as appropriate.**

○ 1. Is the essay correctly formatted with indented paragraphs?

○ 2. Does the introduction include a hook, background information, and a thesis statement at the end that focuses the topic and prepares the reader for the main action event?

○ 3. Do the paragraphs give enough specific details about the main event?

○ 4. Are the details well organized in a clear sequence?

○ 5. Does the conclusion show what the writer learned from the experience?

○ 6. Does the essay contain a variety of vocabulary?

○ 7. Does the sentence structure support the flow of the story with time adverbs and subordinating conjunctions?

○ 8. Are all the verbs in the correct form?

**Go to the Web to print out a peer editor's worksheet.**

**Test-Taking Tip**

When you finish drafting your essay, read it backwards sentence by sentence. That way you can focus on grammar and not get lost in the ideas. Remember that for a narrative, you'll probably need a lot of past tenses.

**Write a narrative essay on one of the following topics.**

**Computer Science:** Tell the story of how a piece of technology helped you solve a problem. What was your problem? What technology did you use? How did it help? What did you learn?

**Engineering:** Tell the story of an invention. Who was the inventor? How did he or she get the idea for the invention? What did he or she invent? How was it received by the public? (You may want to do some Internet research.)

**Health Science:** Tell the story of an illness that you had. What symptoms did you have? What happened to you? How did you recover? What did you learn about the causes, symptoms, and/or treatments?

**Literary Analysis:** Retell the plot of a story, novel, or movie. Who were the characters? What problems did they face? Describe the events. How were the problems solved? What made the story interesting to you?

**Psychology:** Tell about a time when someone persuaded you to do something you didn't want to do. How did the person persuade you? How did you feel about it? What did you learn from the experience?

# UNIT 4

# Comparison-Contrast Essays

**Academic Focus** | Travel and Tourism

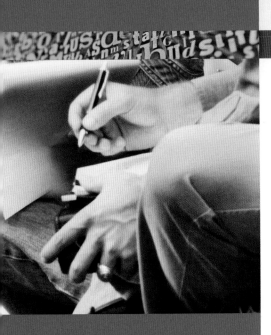

## Unit Goals

### Rhetorical Focus

- comparison-contrast organization

### Language and Grammar Focus

- comparison and contrast connectors
- comparatives in comparison-contrast essays
- comparatives in sentences

A comparison-contrast essay can be used to illustrate the similarities and differences between one idea or image and another. Often these comparisons help us to see the image or idea in a new way.

## Exercise 1 Thinking about the topic

A. Discuss the pictures with a partner.

- Compare the two classroom environments.
- What is the relationship between the teacher and students in each picture?
- What types of classes would suit each environment (for example, engineering, psychology, nursing, literature)?

B. In which of these places would you rather be? Why? Make notes. Then discuss your preferences in small groups.

_____

_____

_____

_____

_____

_____

_____

_____

_____

_____

_____

Sometimes living and working in another place can be quite a shock. In this article, award-winning economist Mohammad Yunus describes his experience as a Ph.D student in the United States.

# Learning about Differences

Despite my success, I still wanted to study and teach. So when I was offered a Fulbright scholarship in 1965, I jumped at the chance to get a Ph.D in the United States. This was my third trip abroad. As a Boy Scout I had gone to Niagara Falls, Canada, in 1955 and to Japan and the Philippines in 1959. But this time I was on my own, and I was in for some surprises.

At first the University of Colorado campus in Boulder was quite a shock. In Bangladesh, students never called professors by their first names. If one spoke to "sir," it was only after being invited by "sir" to speak, and then one spoke in **enormously** respectful terms. But in Boulder, teachers seemed to consider themselves friends of the students. I often saw faculty and students **sprawled out** on the lawn **barefoot**, sharing food, joking, and chatting. Such familiarity was totally unthinkable in Bangladesh. And as for the young female students in Colorado, well, I was so shy and embarrassed I did not know where to look.

At Chittagong College, female students were the minority. Of a student body of eight hundred, no more than one hundred and fifty were women. Women were also **segregated**. They were usually confined to the Women's Common Room, which was off-limits to male students. Their participation in student politics and other activities was limited. When we staged plays, for example, women were not allowed to participate.

My female students at Chittagong University were extremely shy. When it was time for class, they would **huddle** in a group just outside the Teachers' Common Room and then follow me to class, **clutching** their books and looking down at their feet so as to avoid the stares of the boys. Inside the classroom they sat apart from the boys, and I learned not to ask them questions that could possibly embarrass them in front of their classmates. I never talked to them outside the classroom.

Adapted from Yunus, Mohammad. *Banker to the Poor.* New York: Public Affairs, 2007.

**enormously:** extremely
**sprawled out:** sitting or lying in a relaxed manner
**barefoot:** without shoes
**segregated:** separated
**huddle:** stand closely together
**clutching:** holding tightly

## Exercise 3 Understanding the text

**Write *T* for true or *F* for false for each statement.**

_____ 1. This was Yunus' first trip outside of Bangladesh.

_____ 2. The author was surprised by the behavior of students at the University of Colorado.

_____ 3. The author was eager to make friends with his female classmates at the University of Colorado.

_____ 4. At Chittagong University, the author had more direct interaction with the female students than with the male students.

## Exercise 4 Responding to the text

**Respond to the reading by answering the following questions.**

1. How was communication between professors and students different at the University of Colorado than it was at Chittagong University?

_____

_____

_____

2. How did Yunus react to the young female students in Colorado? Why do you think this is so?

_____

_____

_____

3. According to the author, how was the experience of female students at Chittagong University different from that of male students?

_____

_____

_____

4. In this piece, Yunus is writing about an experience that he had in 1965. Has students' behavior changed over the last 40 years? If so, how?

_____

_____

_____

## Exercise 5 Freewriting

**Write for ten to fifteen minutes in your journal. Choose from topics below or an idea of your own. Express your thoughts and feelings. Don't worry about mistakes.**

- What did Yunus learn from his experience? What did it make you think about?
- Write about differences and similarities in places you have visited.
- Write about a travel experience that was not what you expected.
- What is a difference in behavior that you have observed when traveling to a new place?
- Do you think that being in a different place changes people? How?

## In **Writing Process Step 2** you will . . .

- learn about comparison-contrast organization.
- brainstorm ideas and specific vocabulary to use in your writing.
- determine the audience and purpose for your comparison-contrast essay.
- create an outline for your essay.

**WRITING TASK** When people travel to other countries, they see many differences in culture. However, people don't necessarily have to travel abroad to find changes in culture. Within a single country there are many differences. In this unit, you will write a comparison-contrast essay about two places. Go to the Web to use the Online Writing Tutor.

## Exercise 1 Brainstorming ideas

**A. Look at this Venn diagram and answer the questions below.**

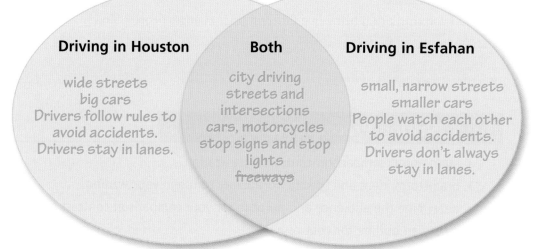

**Driving in Houston**

wide streets
big cars
Drivers follow rules to
avoid accidents.
Drivers stay in lanes.

**Both**

city driving
streets and
intersections
cars, motorcycles
stop signs and stop
lights
~~freeways~~

**Driving in Esfahan**

small, narrow streets
smaller cars
People watch each other
to avoid accidents.
Drivers don't always
stay in lanes.

1. The writer identifies four differences. What are they? _____

_____

2. Why do you think the writer crossed out freeways? _____

_____

3. After looking at the diagram, which is more interesting: the similarities or the

differences? Why? _____

_____

**B. Think of a topic that allows you to compare two places. Narrow your focus by identifying specific locations such as two parks or two airports. Then on a separate piece of paper, create your own Venn diagram. Use the diagram to list the characteristics that are unique to each place, as well as their common characteristics.**

## Exercise 2 Identifying audience and purpose

**A. Circle the best answer to each question. Choose only one.**

1. Who might be interested in your topic?

   a. tourists          b. immigrants          c. business travelers

2. Why might they be reading your essay?

   a. entertainment          b. information          c. advice

3. What is most important for your reader to learn?

   a. mainly similarities          b. mainly differences          c. both

4. How do you want your reader to feel?

   a. motivated          b. satisfied          c. surprised

**B. On a separate piece of paper, write about your goals for the essay.**

## Exercise 3 Brainstorming vocabulary

**A. Match the verb on the left with a noun on the right. Sometimes more than one answer is possible.**

| Verbs | Nouns |
|---|---|
| 1. __c__ enjoy | **a.** an adventure |
| 2. _____ study | **b.** scenery |
| 3. _____ follow | **c.** local food |
| 4. _____ explore | **d.** traditions |
| 5. _____ have | **e.** people |
| 6. _____ meet | **f.** museums |
| 7. _____ sample | **g.** history |
| 8. _____ tour | **h.** nature |

**B. Practice using these word partnerships in sentences. Use your dictionary for help.**

_____

_____

_____

_____

_____

_____

## Comparison-Contrast Organization

A **comparison-contrast essay** uses **points of comparison** to show how two topics in the same category are similar and/or different.

A comparison-contrast essay can focus on similarities, differences, or both, depending on the writer's purpose.

### Introduction

• The introduction presents the subject that is to be compared or contrasted and provides background information that helps the reader understand the writer's point of view.

• The introduction ends with a thesis statement that focuses the essay.

### Body Paragraphs

• The body paragraphs have clear topic sentences that communicate whether the controlling idea will focus on similarities or differences.

• Each topic sentence is followed by supporting ideas about both topics.

• The topics being compared are addressed in the same order for clarity.

### Conclusion

• The conclusion summarizes the differences and similarities. The writer draws a conclusion based on the information presented in the body paragraphs.

**Go to the Web for additional patterns of organization.**

## Exercise 4 Reading a student essay

Read the essay. What two cities does the writer compare?

# A Bi-Cultural Driver

When I first moved to Houston, Texas, I was nervous about driving. The cars were huge, and the streets were wide. I didn't want to get lost in a strange neighborhood, and I did not like going fast. Eventually, I got my American driver's license and became more comfortable with the strange city traffic. I learned to drive naturally in Houston, and life got easier. However, I was very surprised when I returned to Iran after three years. I discovered that I was afraid to drive in Esfahan, my own hometown. I had forgotten that there are major differences between driving in the United States and driving in Iran.

The differences start with the way the streets are organized. In Esfahan, everything looks smaller. Many of the streets are narrow because they used to be alleys for walking. When buildings were torn down, city planners used the space to make room for cars, but there is still not very much room. Fortunately, the cars are usually smaller too, so they can fit in these smaller streets. In Houston, the streets are very wide. Sometimes they have six lanes. There are special lanes for turning left and right. Even the traffic lights are bigger because they have a lot of arrows. These arrows give drivers permission to make left turns.

The biggest difference is the way the drivers behave in each place. Esfahani drivers pay attention to other drivers but not the rules. Cars move from lane to lane so much that they look like fish trying to push their way down a river. When the traffic is not moving very fast, Esfahani drivers will go through a red light without stopping, and they do not wait for a light to make a left turn. While drivers honk at the cars turning left, they are not surprised. These drivers do the same thing when they turn, so they know what to expect.

In contrast to drivers in Esfahan, Houston drivers almost always follow the rules, but they do not pay as much attention to other drivers. Houstonians stay in their lanes or use their signals when they want to change lanes. They stop and wait for a turn signal or a green light, and they always stop at stop signs, even when there are no other drivers around. They are very surprised when other drivers do not follow the traffic rules, and they get angry if they see other drivers driving between lanes.

When I returned to Iran, I discovered that I had changed. I was more like a Houston driver. I was waiting for people to follow the signals, and I did not pay attention to other drivers. I almost got into an accident. However, after a couple of weeks, my old habits started to come back, and I was able to drive Esfahani style once again. Now I feel proud that I am a bi-cultural driver. I know the language of the road in Iran and in the United States.

## Exercise 5 Examining the student essay

**A. Respond to the essay by answering the following questions.**

1. Why is the writer surprised when he returns to his hometown?

_____

_____

2. What useful travel information does the writer share?

_____

_____

3. Why does the writer focus on city streets and not highways?

_____

_____

4. Does the writer believe that one way to drive is better than another? Explain.

_____

_____

_____

**B. Examine the organization of the essay. Answer the questions below.**

1. In which paragraph do you learn the writer's background knowledge for comparing

   the two places? _____

2. Underline the thesis statement twice. Does it tell how the essay will be organized?

   _____

3. Underline the topic sentences of the body paragraphs. What is the focus of each?

   _____

   _____

4. Does the writer mention both cities in each paragraph? _____

5. What conclusion does the writer draw? Do you agree with it? _____

_____

## Exercise 6 Writing an outline

GO ONLINE

**Review your brainstorming ideas and your freewriting exercise. Then go to the
Web to print out an outline template for your essay.**

In **Writing Process Step 3** you will . . .

- learn about comparison-contrast connectors.
- write a first draft of your comparison-contrast essay.

## Exercise 1 Reading a student essay

Read the essay. Which city does the author prefer?

## My Two Homes

There are two places that have had a profound impact in my life. One of them is New York City, where I live now, and the other is Quetzaltenango, Guatemala, where I was born and lived the first part of my life. When you compare them, they seem like dramatically different places, but they have some things in common, and I love them both.

There are many reasons why New York seems like my home away from home. Both cities are striking and distinctive. For example, each has its own nickname. Everyone knows New York is "the Big Apple." Quetzaltenango is known as "Xela" (pronounced shey-la), which is a lot easier to say! Second, both cities have a "Central Park" where people like to go and walk. Although Central Park in Xela is smaller, its tropical flowers and colonial architecture make it just as beautiful as New York's. Furthermore, when you walk around Xela, you find many tourists and people from other countries, just like in New York. For me, this means conversations in Xela are just as interesting as conversations in New York.

Despite their similarities, these cities are different. Life in Xela is more colorful, and the pace of life is slower. For this reason, whenever I return to Xela, it is like an escape. When I arrive, the first thing I notice is the color. In New York, many people wear black to be stylish, but in Xela stylish clothing is the rainbow-colored clothing of the indigenous people. And because Xela is smaller, the beautiful green mountains outside the city are always visible. The second thing I notice is the pace of life. They say New York never sleeps, and it must be true, because I always see people walking and cars on the streets, even late at night. Unlike

New York, my Guatemalan city definitely sleeps. A few families take a walk
in the city's Central Park, but by ten o'clock the streets are pretty deserted.
In Xela people eat their breakfast at home, and most come home from work
for a much more relaxed and longer lunch. In contrast, New Yorkers are
often in such a hurry that they don't even stop to eat. For breakfast they
buy food on the street and eat it while they are walking or on the subway.
At lunch they order food from work and eat at their desks.

In conclusion, these are the two cities I love. For me, both are home,
both are unique, and both are filled with interesting people. These
places represent the best of both worlds. New York is more hurried and
rushed when I need energy, and Xela gives me a slower pace when I
need to relax. Together they keep me balanced.

## Exercise 2 Examining the student essay

**Examine the essay by responding to the questions and statements below. Compare
your answers with a partner.**

1. What two places does the author compare? _____

2. Circle the thesis statement.

3. What do the two places have in common? _____

_____

_____

4. Re-read the second body paragraph. What details support the two points of
   contrast mentioned in the topic sentence of the paragraph?

   • Point of contrast 1 (color): _____

   _____

   • Point of contrast 2 (pace of life): _____

   _____

5. Look at the conclusion. In your own words, describe the writer's feelings about
   the two places. _____

   _____

   _____

## Comparison-Contrast Connectors

In comparison-contrast essays, **connectors** help create coherence by indicating the relationship between ideas in sentences.

### Connectors That Show Similarity

Use connectors such as *like* (+ noun phrase) or *similarly* to show similarity.

> **Like** her sister, Angela was very tall.
>
> I grew up overseas in Shanghai. **Similarly**, my wife spent her childhood abroad in Laos.

### Connectors That Show Contrast

Use connectors like *unlike* (+ noun phrase) or *in contrast* to show contrast.

> **Unlike** my father, I feel shy when I meet new people.
>
> The pace of life in New York is very rapid. **In contrast**, life in Xela is slower.

## Exercise 3 Filling in connectors

**Complete the paragraph. Write** *like, similarly, unlike,* **or** *in contrast* **in the blanks.**

The Eiffel Tower in Paris, France, and the Statue of Liberty in New York City may seem to be very different structures. However, they have many similarities. _____Like_____ the Eiffel

**1.**

Tower, the Statue of Liberty was designed by a French architect.

_____, the Statue of Liberty and Eiffel Tower

**2.**

both represented great advancements in metalwork. The Eiffel Tower, however, is taller than the Statue of Liberty. The Eiffel Tower measures 986 feet. _____, the Statue of

**3.**

Liberty is only 305 feet from the water to the top of her torch.

_____ the elegant black frame and sharp point of

**4.**

the Eiffel Tower, the Statue of Liberty has long, flowing robes and a lifelike torch. Both monuments are equally beautiful.

## Exercise 4 Using connectors to compare and contrast

**Rewrite the following sentences to show similarity or contrast. Choose the correct connector in parentheses to add more coherence.**

1. Lemons are yellow. Limes are green. (unlike / similarly)

   *Unlike lemons, limes are green.*

2. Many families can live in an apartment building. Only one or two families usually live in a house. (in contrast / like)

   _____

3. A frog can live in water or on land. A fish cannot. (like / unlike)

   _____

4. In Dubai, people eat a lot of rice. Korean families serve rice at most meals. (similarly / in contrast)

   _____

5. Rome is rich in history. Athens has thousands of years of civilization. (like / in contrast)

   _____

6. Mozart composed his first opera at the age of 12. Mendelssohn composed his first masterpiece in his teens. (in contrast / similarly)

   _____

## Exercise 5 Writing a first draft

GO ONLINE

**Review your outline and look back at the writing task. Then write the first draft of a comparison-contrast essay on an aspect of two places. Go to the Web to use the Online Writing Tutor.**

## Exercise 6 Peer editing a first draft

A. After writing a first draft, it is helpful to get feedback on your ideas. Exchange essays with two other people. For each essay you read, answer the Peer Editor's Questions on a separate piece of paper. Then discuss your responses.

GO ONLINE

## Peer Editor's Questions

1. What is your favorite part of the essay?

2. What questions do you have about the background?

3. Who do you think will be interested in reading this essay? Why?

4. Are the similarities and differences clearly described?

5. Review the conclusion. What does it make you think about?

**Go to the Web to print out a peer editor's worksheet.**

B. Review your feedback and the organization guidelines on page 86. Make notes for your revision. In this step, you may add, remove, or rewrite information to clarify your ideas.

In **Writing Process Step 4** you will . . .

- learn about using comparatives in comparison-contrast essays.
- learn to use comparatives in sentences.
- edit your first draft and write a second draft.

Now that you have written your first draft, it is time to edit. Editing involves making changes to your writing to improve it and to correct mistakes.

GO ONLINE

## Language and Grammar Focus

### Using Comparatives in Comparison-Contrast Essays

Comparison-contrast essays often use **comparatives**. Comparatives are used with adjectives, adverbs, and nouns to show differences between two subjects (people, objects, ideas, places, or actions).

#### Comparatives with Adjectives and Adverbs

To form the comparative of one-syllable adjectives and adverbs, add -er. If the adjective or adverb ends in a single vowel and consonant, double the consonant.

To form the comparative of most two-syllable adjectives and adverbs, add *more*; however, if the adjective ends in -le, use -r. If the adjective ends in a consonant + y, change y to i and add -er.

#### Comparatives with Nouns

To form the comparative of nouns, use *more*.

## Comparative Forms of Adjectives, Adverbs, and Nouns

| ADJECTIVES | | |
|---|---|---|
| **ONE SYLLABLE** | **TWO SYLLABLES** | **THREE OR MORE SYLLABLES** |
| tall   tall**er** | simple   simpl**er** | beautiful   **more** beautiful |
| cold   cold**er** | happy   happi**er** | expensive   **more** expensive |
| cute   cut**er** | famous   **more** famous | creative   **more** creative |
| big   bigg**er** | polite   polit**er** / **more** polite | intelligent   **more** intelligent |

| ADVERB REGULAR FORMS | |
|---|---|
| **ONE SYLLABLE** | **TWO SYLLABLES** |
| hard   hard**er** | quickly   **more** quickly |
| late   lat**er** | clearly   **more** clearly |

| ADVERB IRREGULAR FORMS | | |
|---|---|---|
| **ADJECTIVE** | **ADVERB** | **COMPARATIVE** |
| good | well | **better** |
| bad | badly | **worse** |

| NOUNS | | | |
|---|---|---|---|
| **COUNT NOUN** | **COMPARATIVE** | **NONCOUNT NOUN** | **COMPARATIVE** |
| a book | **more** books | homework | **more** homework |

## Exercise 1 Forming comparatives

Write the comparative form of the following adjectives and adverbs, using *-er* or *more*.

1. difficult            <u>more difficult</u>

2. challenging        _____

3. smart                  _____

4. tired                   _____

5. sleepy                 _____

6. energetically       _____

7. humble               _____

GO ONLINE

## Language and Grammar Focus

### Using Comparatives in Sentences

When we use a comparative in a sentence, we sometimes delete the second subject and verb. We also sometimes use the comparative without *than* when the context is clear. Look at the examples and charts below.

People in Xela are **less** stressed <u>than New Yorkers are</u>.
New Yorkers are always rushing around. People in Xela are **less** stressed.

### Comparatives in Sentences

| COMPARATIVES WITH *THAN* AND SUBJECTS | | | |
|---|---|---|---|
| | COMPARATIVE | *THAN* | SUBJECT (+ VERB OR AUXILIARY) |
| Lisa is | **taller** | | **her brother (is).** |
| Tony works | **harder** | **than** | **you (work).** <br> **she (does).** |
| We read | **more books** | | **our neighbors (do).** |

| COMPARATIVES WITH *THAN* AND OBJECT PRONOUNS | | | |
|---|---|---|---|
| | COMPARATIVE | *THAN* | OBJECT PRONOUN |
| Lisa is | **taller** | | **him.** |
| Tony works | **harder** | **than** | **you.** |
| We read | **more books** | | **them.** |

## Exercise 2 Identifying comparatives

**Underline the comparative in the sentences below.**

1. Time passes <u>more slowly</u> in Xela <u>than</u> it does in New York.
2. The airport in Dubai is more elegant than the airport in Los Angeles.
3. Shanghai has more skyscrapers than Sydney.
4. The drivers in Houston are more cautious than the Esfahani drivers.
5. Cairo has more tourists than Alexandria.
6. The buildings around Central Park are taller than the museums and houses that surround Chapultapec Park.

## Exercise 3 Choosing the correct form of comparatives

**Circle the correct form of the comparative in each sentence.**

1. She was (very excited / more excited) than her sister was about the trip.
2. Franz spoke (more enthusiastic / more enthusiastically) than Cyrus about computer science.
3. Taipai is much (busier / more busy) than it was a few years ago.
4. In Quetzaltenango the buildings are (older / more old).
5. Tokyo subways (have more passengers / more passengers have).
6. Some tourists think that a beach vacation is (relaxier / more relaxing) than an adventure vacation.

## Exercise 4 Writing comparatives in sentences

**Complete each sentence using a comparative. Use -er, -ier, more, or less.**

1. A skyscraper is _____ taller _____ than a sand dune.

2. Canada is _____ than Singapore.

3. A pizzeria is _____ than a four-star restaurant.

4. A soccerball is _____ than a tennis ball.

5. A hospital is _____ than a medical clinic.

6. A library is _____ than a bookstore.

## Exercise 5 Editing a paragraph

**Read the paragraph. Find and correct six more mistakes with comparatives.**

My old home is very different from where I live now. My old home was
a house, but my new home is an apartment. My new apartment is ~~more~~
*smaller*
~~small~~ than my old house, but the rooms are more large. Everyone in my
family feels differently about this. My parents liked my old house because
it was spaciouser, but I like the apartment because my room is more big.
My brothers don't like the new apartment so much because they have to
share a room. My older brother is more independent my younger brother,
so he wants his own room. My new apartment is also more close to the
bus stop, so it is convenient than my old house, but it is also noisier.

## Exercise 6 Editing your first draft and rewriting

Review your essay for mistakes. Use the checklist below. Then write a final draft.
Go to the Web to use the Online Writing Tutor.

GO ONLINE

### Editor's Checklist

**Put a check (✓) as appropriate.**

CONTENT AND ORGANIZATION

○ 1. Does your thesis statement compare two topics?

○ 2. Does each body paragraph have a clear topic sentence and support?

○ 3. Do you have connectors to show similarities or differences?

LANGUAGE

○ 4. Did you use comparatives correctly in your essay?

**Go to the Web to print out a peer editor's worksheet.**

 In **Review** you will . . .

• review the use of connectors and comparatives in comparison-contrast writing.

# Review | Putting It All Together

**In Putting It All Together you will review what you learned in this unit.**

## Exercise 1 Using connectors to compare and contrast

**Rewrite the following sentences using the correct connector in parentheses to add more coherence. Change sentences to phrases as necessary.**

1.  Vitamin C is water soluble. Vitamin D is not water soluble. (unlike / similarly)

    Unlike Vitamin D, Vitamin C is water soluble.

2.  Chemists work in labs. Biologists do research in labs. (in contrast / similarly)

    _____

3.  CDs record only sound. DVDs contain sound and video. (unlike / like)

    _____

4.  A river is long and thin. A lake is wider, and usually deeper. (similarly / in contrast)

    _____

5.  A fish can be an easy pet. A bird needs a lot of attention. (similarly / in contrast)

    _____

6.  A friend can help you when you have problems. A brother or sister can, too.
    (like / unlike)

    _____

## Exercise 2 Forming comparatives

**Write the comparative form of the following adjectives and adverbs, using -er or *more*.**

1.  fast          _____

2.  pretty        _____

3.  exciting      _____

4.  terrible      _____

5.  well          _____

6.  spicy         _____

## Exercise 3 **Identifying comparatives**

**Underline the comparative in the sentences below.**

1. Computers today are more reliable than they were ten years ago.
2. Cars also run faster than they used to.
3. People today watch more TV than they did in the past.
4. Communication is more rapid than it once was.
5. Phones are smarter than they were just a few years ago.
6. People can communicate more easily now than they could in the past.

## Exercise 4 **Editing a paragraph**

**Read the paragraph and edit as necessary. There are six mistakes with comparatives.**

I like to go on public transportation whenever I can. Of course, private transportation is more comfortable public transportation in many ways. But I always feel more free when I travel on a bus or a train. I don't have to worry about parking, and I can still go wherever I want. Also, taking buses and trains is interestinger. You meet more people and can spend more time enjoying the scenery. For me, this is much more relaxing driving my own car. I also find that I travel more light when I don't have my car, so life is more simpler than when I have lots and lots of suitcases and things to carry.

In **Timed Writing** you will . . .

• practice writing with a time limit.

Practice your test-taking skills with the following practice topic. Read the prompt. Then follow the steps below.

> Customers know that there are different types of salespeople. Some salespeople are successful and others are not. Write a comparison-contrast essay about two salespeople who have influenced your purchasing decisions.

## Step 1  BRAINSTORMING: 5 minutes

Write down ideas and vocabulary for your essay on a separate piece of paper. You may want to use a Venn diagram to do this.

## Step 2  OUTLINING: 5 minutes

Write an outline for your essay. Use another piece of paper if necessary.

| Introduction (First Paragraph) | |
| --- | --- |
| **Hook**<br>Use a personal story or a surprising statement to engage your reader. | |
| **Background Information**<br>Tell where the information about the topics came from or why it is important. | |
| **Thesis Statement**<br>Introduce the topics, and tell how they will be compared. | |
| **Body Paragraphs (Middle Paragraphs)** | |
| **Topics and Controlling Ideas**<br>Introduce your main points of comparison and identify details. | |
| **Conclusion (Last Paragraph)** | |
| **Summary and Comment**<br>Summarize the main points and draw a conclusion based on the comparison in the body paragraphs. | |

**WRITING:** 40 minutes

Use your brainstorming notes and outline to write your essay on a separate piece of paper.

**EDITING:** 10 minutes

When you have finished your essay, check it for mistakes using this checklist.

**GO ONLINE**

## Editor's Checklist

**Put a check (✓) as appropriate.**

- ○ 1. Does the thesis statement compare two subjects?
- ○ 2. Does each body paragraph include details to support the topic sentence?
- ○ 3. Does the essay include connectors to add coherence?
- ○ 4. Does the essay use the correct form of comparatives?
- ○ 5. Does the conclusion summarize the points of comparison and/or contrast?

**Go to the Web to print out a peer editor's worksheet.**

**Test-Taking Tip**

After you finish your Venn diagram, read the prompt again to make sure you are answering the prompt. Again, after you finish drafting, check the draft against the prompt. These steps help ensure that you are responding in the way the testers are expecting.

**Write a comparison-contrast essay on one of the following topics.**

**Education:** What makes a good teacher? Compare two good teachers that you have had. What were the similarities and differences between them? What conclusion can you draw about effective teaching?

**Engineering:** Compare two national monuments (e.g., statues, war memorials, buildings). Where are they, and what do they represent? When and how were they built? With what? Were they successful? Why?

**Hospitality:** Compare two restaurants that serve the same type of food. What points of comparison do you use when you decide on a restaurant? Use those points of comparison to evaluate the restaurants.

**Marketing:** Compare two vehicles designed for the same market. What is the market? What is important to potential buyers? How do the vehicles fit or not fit the buyers' needs?

**Urban Studies:** Compare two neighborhoods that you know. How are they similar or different in effectively meeting the needs of residents?

# UNIT 5 Opinion Essays

## Unit Goals

### Rhetorical Focus

- opinion organization
- facts and opinions
- counter-argument and refutation

### Language and Grammar Focus

- quantity expressions in opinion essays
- connectors to show support and opposition

Some people like change, whereas others prefer traditional ways of living and doing things. In this unit, you will critically analyze a technology and give an opinion about whether it is beneficial or harmful to society.

## Exercise 1 Thinking about the topic

**A. Discuss the picture with a partner.**

- Describe the picture.
- Where is the man?
- What is he doing?
- In what ways do you think his life is different from his parents' lives?

**B. Make a list of technologies that have changed the way people live. Then discuss in small groups.**

_____

_____

_____

_____

_____

_____

This article discusses wireless communication in Bhutan, a country high in the mountains of Asia that has a traditional way of life.

# Wireless Technology in the Land of the Thunder Dragon

There may be no traffic lights in Thimpu, the capital of Bhutan, but there is wireless Internet. The Bhutanese tried traffic lights, but soon **got rid of** them. People did not like the **impersonal** flashing lights, so they went back to a traffic officer in white gloves. This **selectivity** is just one example of how the Bhutanese are handling a difficult transition in their society. They have begun introducing modern technology while carefully guarding their thousand-year-old way of life.

For many years, geography and politics helped to maintain Bhutan's **isolation**. This **sparsely** populated democracy is high in the Himalayan mountains between India and China. Most of it is protected forest, and many villages are not **accessible** by roads. Nearly 70 percent of the population work in agriculture. Also, only a few tourists are allowed to visit every year. These tourists can easily be spotted among the Bhutanese, who dress in traditional clothing.

Today, however, a need for increased access to medicine has set the country on track to modernize its health-care system. Faced with a shortage of hospitals, doctors, and money, leaders have skipped many of the traditional steps to building **infrastructure**. Rather than building roads and **landlines,** they have gone straight to wireless technology.

Today doctors in Bhutan's remote villages use wireless technology to send their harder cases, along with X-rays and other supporting material, to Japan, India, and other countries. Experts in those countries evaluate the cases and send back treatment suggestions. In less than half the time it would take to send a patient to a hospital by ambulance (Twenty or more hours in many instances), the village doctor is able to treat the patient.

While wireless technology has brought improvements to medical care and education, it has also brought other changes. Some people worry about the cultural effects that foreign media and music will have in the Land of the Thunder Dragon, as the Bhutanese call their country. Already changes in dress and behavior are evident, changes that may not be as easy to get rid of as a traffic light.

**got rid of:** removed something not wanted
**impersonal:** without human warmth and attention
**selectivity:** choice of some things and not others
**isolation:** separateness from other places or things
**sparsely:** small in numbers, often spread out over a large area
**accessible:** easy to reach or get
**infrastructure:** systems and services that help a country work effectively
**landlines:** traditional telephone lines

## Exercise 3 Understanding the text

**Write *T* for true or *F* for false for each statement.**

_____ 1. The Bhutanese capital is not a typical modern city.

_____ 2. The Bhutanese want to modernize by cutting down their forests.

_____ 3. Wireless technology allows doctors to improve their services to patients.

_____ 4. It is easy to stop the influence of the Internet on young Bhutanese people.

## Exercise 4 Responding to the text

**Respond to the reading by answering the following questions.**

1. How does wireless technology help the mountainous country of Bhutan save money on infrastructure? _____

   _____

2. Why is it important for Bhutan (or any country) to keep traditions? _____

   _____

3. In your opinion, why are young people more affected by foreign media and music than older generations? _____

   _____

4. The Bhutanese got rid of their impersonal traffic lights. What technologies would you like to get rid of in your community? Why? _____

   _____

## Exercise 5 Freewriting

Write in your journal for ten to fifteen minutes about positive and negative effects of technology. Choose a technology from the box below or an idea of your own. Write about how the technology has changed the world.

| | |
|---|---|
| **Communications** | smart phones, apps, messaging, social networks |
| **Energy** | oil, solar, wind, nuclear, hydroelectric (dams) |
| **Medicine** | diagnostic machines, biotechnology, vaccines |
| **Transportation** | electric cars, driverless cars, high-speed trains |
| **Other** | robotics, design software, computer games, online classes |

- What is it?
- Who uses it?
- How does it benefit people? What problem does it solve?
- What are the negative effects or drawbacks, such as cost?
- How has it changed people's lives?
- What do you want people to realize about it?

## In **Writing Process Step 2** you will . . .

- learn about opinion organization.
- brainstorm ideas and specific vocabulary to use in your writing.
- determine the audience and purpose for your opinion essay.
- create an outline for your essay.

**WRITING TASK** Technology can improve lives, but it can also create new problems in society. In this unit, you will write an opinion essay about a controversy involving technology and how it affects individuals, families, and/or society. Go to the Web to use the Online Writing Tutor.

## Exercise 1 Brainstorming ideas

A. Read the opinions presented in the chart below. Which opinion do you agree with? Fill in the chart with additional reasons to support your opinion. Compare your answers with a partner.

| Opinion | Issue | Opinion |
|---|---|---|
| Space exploration is important to society and should be funded by the government.<br><br>Space exploration creates new technology:<br><br>computers<br><br>robotics<br><br>satellites<br><br>New inventions help the economy. They make life better. | Space Exploration | Space exploration is an unnecessary expense, and governments should use the money in more beneficial ways.<br><br>education<br><br>health care |

B. Fill in the chart below with positive and negative effects of a technology that interests you. Write reasons for and against the technology. Decide which side you agree with.

| Opinion | Issue | Opinion |
|---|---|---|
|  |  |  |

## Exercise 2 Identifying audience and purpose

A. Review your brainstorming chart. Then answer the questions in the boxes below. Share your ideas with a partner.

| Take a Side | Understand the Situation |
|---|---|
| Choose a side of the controversy. What is your opinion? | What individuals or groups are affected? |
| **Identify an Audience** | **Identify Your Purpose** |
| What individuals or groups have the power to change the situation? | What change in thinking or behavior do you want to encourage? What do you want the people in power to do? |

B. In the graphic organizer below, write notes about who you imagine will be reading your essay and how you can best persuade them.

| Audience | Purpose |
|---|---|
|  |  |

## Exercise 3 Brainstorming vocabulary

**A. Circle the words you would like to use. Add two more words to each set.**

1. **Positive changes:** foster, support, encourage, _____, _____

2. **Negative changes:** hinder, discourage, prevent, _____, _____

3. **Relationships:** influence, alter, react (to), _____, _____

4. **Results:** produce, result in, bring about, _____, _____

**B. On a separate piece of paper, practice using these words in sentences. Use your dictionary for help.**

## Rhetorical Focus

### Opinion Organization

In an **opinion essay,** the writer tries to convince the reader of a point of view on a controversial issue (something that people disagree about).

#### Introduction
- The hook introduces a controversial issue.

- The hook may be an anecdote, a question, or a surprising statement or fact that makes the reader want to know more.

- The middle sentences explain why the issue is important by giving background information. This background information explains the issue with details about the history or the people involved, what they want, or how it affects them.

- The thesis statement at the end presents the writer's point of view.

#### Body Paragraphs
- The topic sentences support the writer's main argument in the thesis.

- The following sentences support the topic sentence with reasons, facts, and explanations to help the reader understand the writer's point of view.

- The final body paragraph often includes the opposing opinion. This is called the **counter-argument.** The writer then argues against the counter-argument. This is called **a refutation.** In the refutation, the writer points out weaknesses in the counter-argument and shows how his or her own argument is stronger.

#### Conclusion
- The conclusion restates the writer's opinion but often using different, more persuasive language.

- The conclusion may also offer a warning, a prediction, or other type of comment that reinforces the writer's viewpoint.

## Exercise 4 Reading a student essay

**Read the essay. What is the writer's opinion of space exploration?**

# What Can Space Exploration Do for Me?

Astronauts have walked on the moon, robots have traveled to Mars, and countries around the world have contributed to the International Space Station. These exciting events have made a difference in ordinary people's lives whether they realize it or not. Space exploration has not only created history, it has also provided many practical benefits for humans here on Earth.

The importance of space programs can be seen in the technology we use every day. Satellite technology allows people to make phone calls, watch TV shows, and listen to radio programs from everywhere on Earth. Also, many of the advances in computer technology were first invented to support space exploration. For example, the National Aeronautics and Space Administration (NASA) has contributed to the creation of software that people use every day in manufacturing and design. Robotic technology is another useful example. Engineers designed robots to work on the International Space Station, but now robots are being developed to do jobs here on Earth.

Even with all these advances, some people say that space exploration is an expensive luxury that takes money away from important programs such as health care and education. However, if they considered how space technology has improved life on Earth, they would see that space exploration is actually important to civilization.

Space exploration creates a need for technological advances. Later, these advances are used in other ways that help people. Wonderful new inventions such as satellites and computers are just a beginning. In the future, space exploration will provide useful and amazing new inventions that we cannot even imagine in the present.

## Exercise 5 Examining the student essay

**A. Respond to the essay by answering the following questions.**

1. Would the writer agree with someone who said that the space program does not help ordinary people? Why or why not? _____

   _____

2. How do humans depend on satellite technology? _____

   _____

3. Do you agree with the writer that your government should spend money on space programs? Why or why not? _____

   _____

**B. Examine the organization of the essay by responding to the questions and statements below. Compare your answers with a partner.**

1. What strategy does the writer use to get the reader's attention?
   a. a statement          b. a story          c. a question

2. Which of the following best summarizes the author's thesis statement?
   a. Space exploration creates history.
   b. Space exploration has improved daily life on Earth.
   c. The technology needed for space exploration can be used in other ways.

3. Circle the topic sentence of the first body paragraph.

4. Underline examples that support the topic sentence.

5. Draw a box around the counter-argument.

## Exercise 6 Writing an outline

GO ONLINE

Review your brainstorming ideas and your freewriting exercise. Then go to the Web to print out an outline template for your essay.

| In **Writing Process Step 3** you will . . . |
| --- |

- learn to use facts and opinions to support your argument.
- learn about counter-arguments and refutation.
- write a first draft of your opinion essay.

## Exercise 1 Reading a student essay

Read the essay. What does the writer want to change about testing?

# Testing in the 21st Century

Before the invention of computers and the Internet, the average classroom was similar to the world outside. People worked at desks, got information from books, and wrote with pencils. However, today the outside world is very different. People can get information anytime and anywhere. They use this information in their work and daily lives. At the same time, most schools don't allow students to use this tool when they are taking tests. This policy needs to change. Clearly, if schools want to prepare students for the future, they need to allow college students to use the Internet when they are taking tests.

Students should have Internet access while they are taking tests because the Internet is the most important tool in the modern world. Like other tools, students need to learn to use the Internet if they want to be successful. For example, an accountant who knows how to get information about tax laws will save clients' money. A doctor who can get correct information about new medicines can help her patients. In addition, information changes quickly. For example, new scientific information replaces old information every day. No human can learn about or remember all the changes, so people are better off if they can look up the newest information. Finally, people are using more information now than in the past. Take today's global economy. Business students need to learn about different markets and products, and they need to know where to get the best information. Having experience using the Internet to get the right information is more helpful than studying textbooks with information that may not be true anymore.

Old-fashioned people say students need to study facts and information and then use their memories to take tests. They say being able to memorize is important. They have a point. Memorizing is useful for some things like poetry, passwords, and people's names. However, it is not realistic to think that memorizing is the main skill for life outside of school. Students will be more qualified if they learn how to use the Internet to get useful new and correct information. Instead, schools can change their tests so that new ways of getting information are part of the test.

In conclusion, the Internet is the most important tool for human beings in the world today. Schools need to stop being afraid of it. Being able to go online during tests is a better way to help college students prepare for the real world.

## Exercise 2 Examining the student essay

**Examine the essay by responding to the questions and statements below.**

1. Underline the hook. Which of the following strategies is used? Circle one.
   a. a story          c. a description
   b. a fact           d. a question

2. What does the writer compare to make a point in the essay's background information? Is the point persuasive?

   _____

   _____

3. Circle the thesis statement. Does the writer give a clear position?

   _____

4. Underline the topic sentence of the first body paragraph.
5. How many main reasons does the writer give in the first body paragraph?

   _____

6. In which paragraph does the writer introduce a counter-argument and refutation?

   _____

7. Which of the following strategies does the writer use in the conclusion?
   a. giving a warning          b. making a suggestion

## Rhetorical Focus

### Facts and Opinions

Writers use both **facts** and **opinions** to support their positions or arguments. They state their opinions and then back them up with facts. The difference between facts and opinions is shown below.

A **fact** is a truth that is scientifically proven or generally accepted.
A smart phone allows the user to access the Internet.

An **opinion** is one point of view among many.
Cell phones are destroying people's privacy.

## Exercise 3 Distinguishing facts and opinions

**Write *F* if the statement is a fact and *O* if it is an opinion.**

_F_ 1. Small airplanes are used in advertising.

____ 2. Solar panels allow users to get energy from sunlight.

____ 3. Many nations are working together to build and maintain the International Space Station.

____ 4. Solar panels are ugly.

____ 5. Online courses are easier than classroom courses.

## Rhetorical Focus

### Interpreting Facts to Support an Opinion

After the writer gives factual examples, she or he then interprets the facts, explaining how they support her or his opinion. Look at the example below, which includes an opinion, factual examples, and an interpretation of the facts.

| Opinion | Animals use language to communicate with each other. |
|---|---|
| Factual Examples | Arctic wolves, for example, communicate the presence of caribou through their howls and barks. Other wolves hear the messages and are able to meet their pack to join the hunt. |
| Interpretation | Clearly, if another animal can understand vocalized messages that tell it the location of food, then that animal is using language. |

## Exercise 4 Interpreting facts to support opinions

**Read each opinion and fact below. Then write a sentence interpreting the fact to support the opinion.**

1. **Opinion:** The Internet takes too much time away from family life.

   **Fact:** The average adult in the United States spends 14 hours per week on the Internet.

   *Those 14 hours could be spent doing family activities, such as gardening,*

   *helping children with homework, or playing games.*

2. **Opinion:** The government is doing an excellent job of protecting athletes from the pressure to use performance-enhancing drugs.

   **Fact:** Athletes are routinely tested for drug use.

   _____

   _____

3. **Opinion:** Going home to have a long lunch is good for a family.

   **Fact:** According to a recent study, people who eat at home report a higher level of satisfaction with life.

   _____

   _____

4. **Opinion:** Phone applications are a good financial investment.

   **Fact:** One out of every four people owns a smart phone.

   _____

   _____

5. **Opinion:** People spend too much money on food.

   **Fact:** Americans eat meals outside the home an average of five times per week.

   _____

   _____

6. **Opinion:** Young people are too dependent on technology.

   **Fact:** In a study of students from five countries on four continents, 80 percent of participants reported feelings of loneliness and anxiety when they stopped using technology for 24 hours.

   _____

   _____

## Counter-Argument and Refutation

To make an opinion essay as persuasive as possible, the writer includes a **counter-argument** and a **refutation.**

The counter-argument is the opposing opinion. It disagrees with the writer's position. By including the counter-argument, the writer shows an understanding of other points of view.

The refutation is the writer's response to the counter-argument. In the refutation, the writer shows why the counter-argument is weak and the writer's position is strong. The refutation may also address doubts the reader may have about the writer's position.

| | |
|---|---|
| **Counter-argument** | Many people think that a child is unhappy without brothers or sisters; however, most only children would disagree with this statement. |
| **Refutation** | An only child receives more attention from parents, gets into fewer fights, and has plenty of social contact with friends and classmates. |

In the above example, the writer raises a counter-argument (that people think children are unhappy without siblings). Then the writer gives a refutation—only children are not unhappy—and then gives reasons to support the argument.

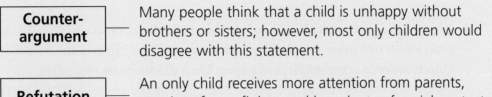

**Exercise 5 Recognizing counter-arguments and refutations**

**Read each statement below. Then underline the counter-argument, and circle the writer's refutation.**

1. Even though many drivers love the power of a big car, smaller cars are the cars of the future.

2. Train travel may be inexpensive and relaxing; however, airplanes are a much more important means of transportation because they are fast and efficient.

3. Most people agree that a traditional home-cooked meal is best, but they have to admit that convenience and low cost is making fast food more popular with students.

4. While some people believe that online courses will never be as popular as traditional classrooms, the demand for online instruction is increasing due to technology, cost, and convenience.

5. Some people criticize credit cards for causing debt; however, it is the irresponsibility of consumers, not credit cards, that causes credit card debt.

6. People often comment that technology makes life easier, but in reality, technology only makes it possible for people to do more work in less time.

## Exercise 6 Writing a first draft

GO ONLINE

**Review your outline. Then write the first draft of an opinion essay on how a technology benefits or harms society. Go to the Web to use the Online Writing Tutor.**

## Exercise 7 Peer editing a first draft

A. After writing a first draft, it is helpful to get feedback on your ideas. Exchange essays with two other people. For each essay you read, answer the Peer Editor's Questions on a separate piece of paper. Then discuss your responses.

GO ONLINE

### Peer Editor's Questions

1. What is your favorite part of the paper?

2. What else would you like to know about the background information in paragraph one?

3. Who do you think will agree with the writer's opinion? Who will disagree? Why?

4. What other information can you think of that the writer might not have thought about?

5. In what ways has the writer made you think about the issue?

**Go to the Web to print out a peer editor's worksheet.**

B. Review your feedback and the organization guidelines on page 110. Make notes for your revision. In this step, you may add, remove, or rewrite information to clarify your ideas.

### In **Writing Process Step 4** you will . . .

- learn about using quantity expressions.
- learn about overgeneralizations.
- learn to use connectors to show support and opposition.
- edit your first draft and write a second draft.

Now that you have written a first draft, it is time to edit. Editing involves making changes to your writing to improve it and to correct mistakes.

**GO ONLINE**

## Language and Grammar Focus

### Using Quantity Expressions in Opinion Essays

In an opinion essay, writers often make general statements. It is important to avoid making a statement that is true for some but not for all members of a group or category. This is called an **overgeneralization.** Compare the following statements.

Cats hate water.     Most cats hate water.

The first statement suggests that all cats in the world hate water. It is untrue because some cats, such as tigers, are good swimmers and enjoy being in water. In the second statement, the writer uses the **quantity expression** *most*. The quantity expression qualifies, or limits the generalization, so that the statement is true.

### Quantity Expressions

The following patterns guide the use of quantity expressions:

• *Most, a lot of,* and *some* are used with both plural count nouns and noncount nouns.
   **Most** dormitories have Internet access.
   **Some** fast food can be healthy.

• *Much* and *a little* are used with noncount nouns. (*Much* is not usually used in affirmative statements. Use *a lot of* instead.)
   Some people have **a lot of** intelligence, but they do not have **much** common sense.
   Students might have **a little** money left for entertainment after paying expenses.

• *Many, several,* and *a few* are used with plural nouns.
   **Many** websites charge a fee for information.
   **A few** uncooperative participants can destroy a meeting.

## Exercise 1 Identifying correct quantity expressions

**Circle the correct quantity expression in each sentence.**

1. (Many / A lot of) creativity is necessary for certain types of technology jobs.

2. There are (a few / a little) places where the sea level is rising.

3. (A little / Several) bills in Congress have tried to protect Internet users from fraud.

4. Only (a little / a few) computer viruses have created serious damage.

5. (Many / A lot of) time is spent doing research on cures for cancer.

6. Did you know that (a little / a few) sleep deprivation can harm a person's judgment?

Using quantity expressions, rewrite the sentences below so that they become more appropriate generalizations.

| | Overgeneralization | Appropriate Generalization |
|---|---|---|
| 1. | Everybody has a TV. | Most people have a TV. |
| 2. | People do not like change. | |
| 3. | People commute to ther jobs. | |
| 4. | Schools are now wireless. | |
| 5. | Medications have side effects. | |
| 6. | New Yorkers love their city. | |
| 7. | Asian countries have hot and humid climates. | |
| 8. | Pollution affects everything. | |

## Language and Grammar Focus

### Using Connectors to Show Support and Opposition

When we explain an opinion, we can use **connectors** to clarify the relationship between ideas. Connectors can be used to signal that the second idea will support the first in some way. They can also be used to contrast the first idea with an opposite or very different idea.

#### Connectors That Show Support

One way to support an idea is to give an example that illustrates the idea. Connectors like *for example* and *in particular* introduce examples.

> Most people are willing to spend money to make their lives easier; for example, most new homes have wireless capabilities.

> Children should avoid junk food; in particular, they should stay away from sugary snacks.

A second way to show support is to add facts or explanations that clarify the idea.

> The automobile industry is responding to consumer demands for more fuel-efficient cars; **in fact,** the number of available models has tripled in the past three years.

#### Connectors That Show Opposition

It is sometimes difficult for the writer to show that two ideas are opposed to each other. Connectors like *however* and *in contrast* help the writer focus the reader's attention on differences.

> Electronic books are becoming more popular; **however,** many people still prefer to read on paper.

> Standard vacations promise relaxation; **in contrast,** extreme tours promise danger and adventure.

When a connector is used to connect two ideas, a semicolon comes before the connector. Then the connector is followed with a comma.

## Exercise 3 Understanding connectors

**Each of the sentences below has two clauses joined by a connector. Write *O* for opposition if the clauses show opposing information or *S* for support if they show supporting information, such as an example or a similar idea.**

__O__ 1. The Western calendar is used around the world; however, many people have a traditional calendar that they also use.

_____ 2. Most people say they want to exercise; however, only one in ten adults works out three times a week or more.

_____ 3. Frank Lloyd Wright was an architect who liked straight lines; in contrast, Antonio Gaudí preferred bends and curves in his designs.

_____ 4. Surgeons try hard to protect their hands; for example, they avoid sports such as baseball that might cause an injury to their fingers.

_____ 5. The place where I grew up only has two seasons; however, my new home, Vancouver, has four.

_____ 6. Computer games can be used to solve real-world problems; in fact, three new games are specifically designed to provide answers to social science questions.

## Exercise 4 Editing a paragraph

**Read the paragraph and edit as necessary. There are three more mistakes in quantity expressions.**

Most working people will agree that traffic congestion creates too much stress. As large cities grow even bigger, there is often so ~~many~~ *much* traffic that people's productivity is reduced. There are two good solutions that could greatly improve traffic conditions in this city. First, high-occupancy vehicle lanes (HOV lanes) are effective. A vehicle can drive in an HOV lane only if the car has at least two passengers. Much workers must begin work at 9:00 every day, so it is easy for them to carpool. If four people ride together, there are three fewer cars on the road. Providing affordable public transportation is another good solution. Much people like to use public transportation because it is cheap and convenient; however, building an effective public transportation system costs many money.

Review your essay for mistakes. Use the checklist below. Then write a final draft. Go to the Web to use the Online Writing Tutor.

**GO ONLINE**

# Editor's Checklist

**Put a check (✓) as appropriate.**

## CONTENT AND ORGANIZATION

○ 1. Does the thesis statement give a clear position on an issue?

○ 2. Does each body paragraph have a clear topic sentence and support?

○ 3. Does the essay use facts to support opinions?

○ 4. Is there a paragraph with a counter-argument and refutation?

○ 5. Does the conclusion provide a convincing suggestion, prediction, or warning?

## LANGUAGE

○ 6. Did you use quantity expressions to avoid generalizations?

○ 7. Did you use connectors to show support and opposition?

**Go to the Web to print out a peer editor's worksheet.**

## In **Review** you will . . .

- review the differences between facts and opinions.
- review counter-arguments and refutations.
- review the use of opposing and supporting connectors.
- identify correct quantity expressions.

**In Putting It All Together you will review what you learned in this unit.**

## Exercise 1 Identifying facts and opinions

**Write *F* if the statement is a fact. Write *O* if it is an opinion.**

_____ 1. The Galápagos tortoise is the largest living tortoise.

_____ 2. People spend too much money on fashion.

_____ 3. Scientists have evidence that birds are capable of complex thought.

_____ 4. It is more fun to be a soccer fan than a soccer player.

_____ 5. The saguaro cactus is the most beautiful of all desert plants.

_____ 6. Bats feed on the fruit of the saguaro cactus, which only blooms at night.

## Exercise 2 Recognizing counter-arguments and refutations

**Read the statements below. Then underline the counter-argument and circle the writer's refutation.**

1. Even though many people say they enjoy visiting bookstores, downloading books from the Internet is becoming increasingly popular.

2. Not very many people actually ride in helicopters, so they might not think about them as important for our society; however, helicopters are necessary for many areas of city life, including news agencies, law enforcement, and emergency medicine.

3. The driverless car is laughed at by many people because they think it is not possible for a car to function without a driver, but new advances in technology may replace drivers with safer, more efficient, driverless vehicles.

4. Day-care centers offer benefits to the children, their parents, and society even though there will always be people who disagree with day-care providers.

5. Many people consider a new type of rice as no big deal; however, the development of rice plants that are strong and resistant to disease can help prevent starvation in many countries.

6. Some people say that traveling to other countries is a waste of money, but international travel is worth the cost because it is fun and educational.

## Exercise 3 Understanding connectors

**Each of the sentences below has two clauses joined by a connector. Write *O* for opposition if the clauses show opposing information or *S* for support if they show supporting information, such as an example or a similar idea.**

_____ 1. Kayaking can be a cold and wet sport; however, many people find it exciting and pleasurable.

_____ 2. A mall is a pleasant place to spend a Saturday afternoon; in fact, many people enjoy spending time at malls even if they are not shopping.

_____ 3. Engineers must be precise in their thinking; in contrast, artists work by freeing their imaginations.

_____ 4. It is true that some people become addicted to exercise; for example, I have a friend who feels anxious if she cannot work out at the gym every day.

_____ 5. A useful future invention would be one that replaces traditional keys and locks with something that recognizes fingerprints; in fact, most people would love this invention because they would not have to worry about losing or forgetting their keys.

_____ 6. Many parents want their children to get university degrees because they worry about their children's careers; however, there are many other ways that young people can become successful.

## Exercise 4 Identifying correct quantity expressions

**Circle the correct quantity expression in each sentence below.**

1. (Many / A lot of) equipment is needed for rock climbing.

2. There will always be (a few / a little) people who resist change.

3. (Some / A little) instructions are so badly written that it is impossible to use them.

4. (A little / Many) allergies can be treated with medication.

5. (Most / Many) job training involves actually doing a task.

6. Offices usually have (a few / a little) space set aside for socializing.

## Exercise 5 Editing a paragraph

**Read the paragraph. Find and correct five mistakes with connectors.**

Immigrants today have an easier life than immigrants of the past because communication and travel make it easier for us to stay connected to our countries. For immigrants, homesickness and culture shock are big problems; in contrast, many people get very depressed if they cannot speak their language or communicate with their parents. In the past, people had letters and the telephone, but letters took a long time and the telephone was very expensive, so people had to wait a long time for communication. For example, now new applications allow today's immigrants to communicate as often as they want for free. These apps have other advantages, too; for example, I can exchange video, photos, or a real-time conversation with friends anywhere in the world. Another advantage for immigrants today is travel. People sometimes visited their countries in the past, but it was a long and expensive trip; in fact, traveling overseas is easier nowadays because there are many flights and the tickets are not too expensive. I know many people who live in the United States, but they go back to their countries for special occasions; however, my friend went back two times last year for two different wedding celebrations. For an immigrant, going back home for a visit is the best cure for homesickness; in contrast, it helps them feel better about living in the new country. Although many people say that an immigrant's life is never easy, I am very glad that I live in these times and not fifty years ago.

In **Timed Writing** you will . . .

• practice writing with a time limit.

Practice your test-taking skills with the following practice topic. Read the prompt. Then follow the steps below.

> Many schools offer participation in sports as part of the curriculum. However, other schools do not. They claim that their job is to teach skills such as reading and math. Write an essay in which you agree or disagree with the following topic: Learning to play sports teaches valuable life skills.

**Step 1** **BRAINSTORMING:** 5 minutes

Write down ideas and vocabulary for your essay on a separate piece of paper. You may want to use a chart similar to the ones on page 108.

**Step 2** **OUTLINING:** 5 minutes

Write an outline for your essay. Use another piece of paper if necessary.

| Introduction (First Paragraph) | |
|---|---|
| **Hook** <br> Get the reader interested with a personal story or a controversial statement. | |
| **Background Information** <br> Provide background details about the controversy. | |
| **Thesis Statement** <br> State your opinion about the controversy. | |
| **Body Paragraphs (Middle Paragraphs)** | |
| **Topic Sentence and Reasons** <br> Write a topic sentence clarifying and focusing your opinion. Write your reasons with supporting details that show why you think your opinion is correct. | |
| **Topic Sentence, Counter-argument, and Refutation** <br> Write a topic sentence that introduces the counter-argument. Then explain why the counter-argument is wrong. | |
| **Conclusion (Last Paragraph)** | |
| **Summary and Comment** <br> Summarize the main points and make a prediction, a warning, or a suggestion as to why your opinion is best. | |

**Step 3**  **WRITING:** 40 minutes

Use your brainstorming notes and outline to write your essay on a separate piece of paper.

**Step 4**  **EDITING:** 10 minutes

When you have finished your essay, check it for mistakes. Use the checklist below.

GO ONLINE

## Editor's Checklist

**Put a check (✓) as appropriate.**

○ 1. Does the introduction include a hook and a thesis?

○ 2. Do the body paragraphs have topic sentences?

○ 3. Do the body paragraphs give reasons and explanations that support the topic sentences?

○ 4. Does the second body paragraph give a counter-argument and a refutation?

○ 5. Does the conclusion refer to the main idea of the essay?

○ 6. Are quantity expressions used to avoid overgeneralizations?

○ 7. Are connectors used to show the relationship (opposition or support) between ideas?

**Go to the Web to print out a peer editor's worksheet.**

### Test-Taking Tip

When you finish, look at the shape of your paragraphs. Do any of them look bigger or smaller than the others? If a paragraph only has a few lines, you might need to add more details. If a paragraph is much longer than others, you might need to break it into two main ideas.

**Write an opinion essay on one of the following topics.**

**Agriculture:** Pesticides are used to kill insects on fruits and vegetables. However, research shows that they can be harmful to people and the environment. Do you think pesticides should be banned? Why or why not?

**Biology:** Scientists can learn a lot by doing experiments on animals, but some people believe that this makes animals suffer. Should scientists be allowed to continue this research?

**Criminal Justice:** In the United States, people have the right to remain silent when they are questioned by police. In your opinion, is this a good law?

**Marine Science:** Humans know very little about the deep ocean. Should governments spend money to explore the ocean and find out more about resources on the ocean floor?

**Travel and Tourism:** Many places are famous and attract a lot of tourists, but tourism changes these places. Is tourism good for a town?

**Urban Studies:** Traffic is a problem everywhere in the world. It creates congestion, pollution, and noise. In response to this problem, some cities charge an expensive congestion tax to cars in downtown areas. Do you agree with this tax?

# UNIT 6

# Cause-and-Effect Essays

## Unit Goals

### Rhetorical Focus

- cause-and-effect organization
- clustering information

### Language and Grammar Focus

- phrasal verbs
- the future with *will*
- *will* with *so that*
- future possibilities with *if* clauses

By analyzing causes, a writer explains why something happens. By analyzing effects, the writer explains the results or outcome of an event. In this unit, you will write a cause-and-effect essay about how a person has grown.

## Exercise 1 Thinking about the topic

A. Discuss the pictures with a partner.

- Describe the scenes.
- What changes have occurred in this place between the times the two pictures were taken?
- How do you think life has changed for the people who live in this place? Why?

B. Make notes about the ways in which people and places can change and develop over time. Are these changes positive? Negative? What causes these changes?

_____

_____

_____

_____

_____

_____

_____

_____

_____

_____

_____

## Exercise 2 Reading about the topic

This passage discusses the causes of poverty.

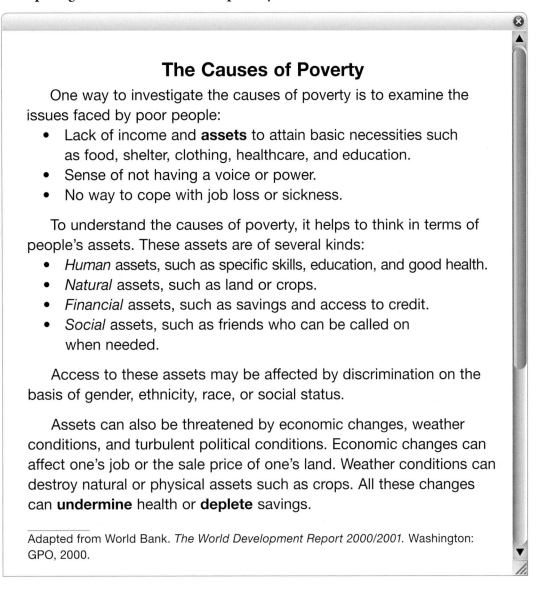

# The Causes of Poverty

One way to investigate the causes of poverty is to examine the issues faced by poor people:

- Lack of income and **assets** to attain basic necessities such as food, shelter, clothing, healthcare, and education.
- Sense of not having a voice or power.
- No way to cope with job loss or sickness.

To understand the causes of poverty, it helps to think in terms of people's assets. These assets are of several kinds:

- *Human* assets, such as specific skills, education, and good health.
- *Natural* assets, such as land or crops.
- *Financial* assets, such as savings and access to credit.
- *Social* assets, such as friends who can be called on when needed.

Access to these assets may be affected by discrimination on the basis of gender, ethnicity, race, or social status.

Assets can also be threatened by economic changes, weather conditions, and turbulent political conditions. Economic changes can affect one's job or the sale price of one's land. Weather conditions can destroy natural or physical assets such as crops. All these changes can **undermine** health or **deplete** savings.

Adapted from World Bank. *The World Development Report 2000/2001.* Washington: GPO, 2000.

**assets:** valuable property or qualities     **deplete:** reduce greatly
**undermine:** damage or weaken

## Exercise 3 Understanding the text

**Write *T* for true or *F* for false for each statement.**

_____ 1. There are multiple causes of poverty.

_____ 2. To understand the causes of poverty, one must only think about what poor people own.

_____ 3. Assets are things of value.

_____ 4. According to the reading, there are three types of assets people can have.

## Exercise 4 Responding to the text

**Respond to the reading by answering the following questions.**

1. What four types of assets does the author list? Which of these assets do you have?

   _____

   _____

2. How are your personal assets valuable to you?

   _____

   _____

3. Which type of asset do you feel is most important? Why?

   _____

   _____

4. What do you feel is the most important asset that you have? Why? What is an asset that you do not have but would like to obtain in the future?

   _____

   _____

## Exercise 5 Freewriting

**Write for ten to fifteen minutes in your journal. Choose from topics below or an idea of your own. Express your thoughts and feelings. Don't worry about mistakes.**

- In the text, the writers list education as a human asset. Write about your own motivations to study.
- What does a person need to do to be good at a sport or to develop an artistic talent?
- What causes someone to leave his or her country to look for opportunities in a different place?
- What leads to a successful job interview?
- What causes people to be successful at learning another language?

### In **Writing Process Step 2** you will . . .

- learn about cause-and-effect organization.
- brainstorm ideas and specific vocabulary to use in your writing.
- determine the audience and purpose for your cause-and-effect essay.
- create an outline for your essay.

**WRITING TASK** Some people say that life is change. In this unit, you will write a cause-and-effect essay about how and why you or another person changed and grew over time. You may choose to discuss personal, professional, educational, or financial growth. Go to the Web to use the Online Writing Tutor.

## Exercise 1 Brainstorming ideas

A. The charts below show cause-and-effect relationships. In the blanks provided, write causes that lead to the particular growth or situation.

| Causes ⟶ | Growth or Situation |
|---|---|
| interesting assignments | |
| a knowledgeable instructor | |
| | a successful class |
| | |
| | |

| Causes ⟶ | Growth or Situation |
|---|---|
| | |
| | |
| | a successful career |
| | |
| | |

B. Think of an event or situation involving personal, professional, educational, or financial growth that you want to write about. Brainstorm the causes that lead to the growth situation and complete the chart below.

| Causes ⟶ | Growth or Situation |
|---|---|
| | |
| | |
| | |
| | |

# Exercise 2 Identifying audience and purpose

**A. For each statement, write *a*, *b*, or *c* to indicate the audience to which each statement would most likely be made.**

1. _____ My main interest in engineering is working on water purification systems.
   _____ I want to study engineering because it is interesting to me.
   _____ We need well-trained engineers to develop systems to provide clean water in rural villages.

   **a.** an employment interview board
   **b.** the leader of a country
   **c.** a parent

2. _____ You need to clean your room.
   _____ Clean rooms prevent the spread of germs.
   _____ The cleanliness of the rooms was really impressive.

   **a.** attendees at a health seminar
   **b.** someone reading a hotel review
   **c.** a child

3. _____ As the city grew, it offered people more educational and professional opportunities.
   _____ I want to move to the city because I will have more employment opportunities.
   _____ As cities grow, more hospitals and schools must be built to serve more inhabitants.

   **a.** architecture students
   **b.** history students
   **c.** a friend

**B. For each audience below, write a sentence about how the person you will write about in your essay has grown and why.**

1. a potential employer

   _____

   _____

2. a friend

   _____

   _____

## Exercise 3 Brainstorming vocabulary

**A. Think about the type of personal development you want to write about. Add two more words to each set. Circle the words that you would like to use.**

1. **Success:** fame, power, status, _____, _____
2. **Actions:** succeed, accomplish, master, _____, _____
3. **Qualities:** dedication, perseverance, creativity, _____, _____
4. **Results:** bring about, result in, contribute to, _____, _____

**B. On a separate piece of paper, practice using the words in sentences. Use your dictionary for help.**

## Rhetorical Focus

### Cause-and-Effect Organization

A **cause-and-effect essay** explains why something happens. Both causes and effects are examined in longer essays. For now, we will focus only on causes that lead to an event or situation.

#### Introduction

- The hook engages the reader's interest. It personalizes the topic or shows why it is important for the reader to know about it.

- The middle sentences describe the event or situation that is the result of the causes. This background information helps the reader understand the relationship between the causes and the effects.

- The thesis statement at the end of the introduction states the causes that lead up to the event or situation. It may also include a comment by the writer that explains why it is important to understand the causes.

#### Body Paragraphs

- The body paragraphs support the thesis statement by explaining the causes in detail.

- Each body paragraph begins with a topic sentence that states one cause for the event or situation.

- The sentences that follow support the idea in the topic sentence. These supporting sentences include details such as examples, descriptions, reasons, and facts to help the reader understand the relationship between the cause and the event.

#### Conclusion

- The conclusion restates the thesis statement using different words and language.

- The conclusion summarizes the main causes and their relationship to the event.

- The conclusion may include a comment by the writer that explains why it is important to understand the causes of the event.

Read the essay. According to the writer, what are the three main ways his parents motivated him to do better?

# Better Than Us

When I was growing up, my family had very little money. My father worked as a construction worker when he could find work, and my mother worked part-time doing laundry in other people's houses. The message from my parents was always clear. They wanted me to have a better life than they had. They wanted me to have a career and be a professional. My parents worked hard and watched over my education and nutrition so I would attain this goal.

Both my parents worked hard and long hours to pay for my studies when I was a child. At one time my father worked in another city far from our home. It was hard for him to be away, but the job offered him a higher salary than at home, so he took it. My mother often worked in more than one house, doing cleaning and laundry. When she had to work late or on the weekend, she asked a neighbor to take care of me. Sometimes she worked seven days a week.

From the time I was very young, my mother did her best to make sure I had good nutrition and a healthy diet. This was not easy with little money. When she could not afford meat she bought grains and cereals that would keep me strong and help me grow. Sometimes my mother ate less so that she could give me more to eat. She always made sure I ate something for breakfast in the morning so I would be able to concentrate more in school.

When I got home from school, I knew it was time to complete my homework. My parents were not always there, but I knew that they would check my homework when they came home. In the mornings when my mother dropped me off at school, she always spoke with my teacher to see if I was having problems. Whenever my mother had time or was not working, she would always go visit my school to see how I was doing.

My parents told me how important it was to study and do better. They motivated me. I have never forgotten their example; it is the most important lesson I have learned in my life. They told me, "When you get an education, you will get a job. Then you will show everyone that you are better than us."

## Exercise 5 Examining the student essay

**A. Respond to the essay by answering the following questions.**

1. Look at the first paragraph of the essay. How was your experience growing up similar to or different from that of the writer's?

   _____

   _____

2. Why did the writer's parents work hard at their jobs?

   _____

   _____

3. How did the mother make sure that the writer ate well? Why did she do this?

   _____

   _____

4. How did the writer's parents make sure he got a good education?

   _____

   _____

5. How do you think the writer feels about what his parents taught him?

   _____

   _____

**B. Examine the organization of the essay by responding to the questions and statements below. Compare your answers with a partner.**

1. How does the writer catch the reader's attention?

   a. with an example that the reader is familiar with

   b. with a surprising fact or statistic

   c. with a short narrative to set the context

2. Put a check (✓) next to the background information that appears in the introduction.

   _____ a. what jobs the writer had

   _____ b. what the writer studied

   _____ c. what the writer's family's economic situation was

3. How many causes will be discussed, according to the thesis statement? _____

4. Does the thesis statement directly state what the causes are? _____

5. Underline the topic sentences of each body paragraph.

6. Fill in the bubbles with three examples from the text that show how the writer supports the topic sentences below.

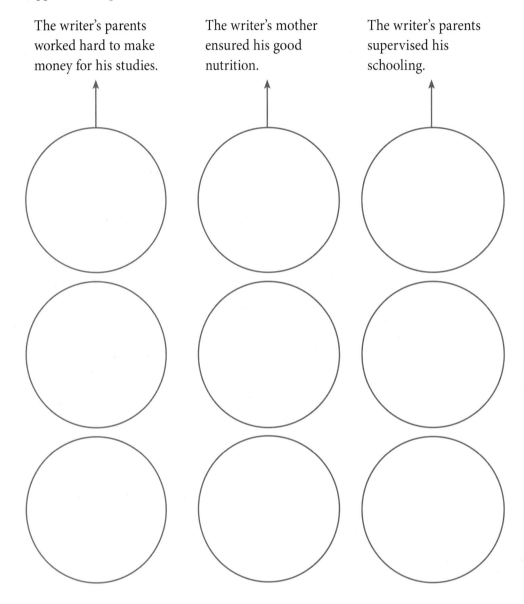

The writer's parents worked hard to make money for his studies.

The writer's mother ensured his good nutrition.

The writer's parents supervised his schooling.

## Rhetorical Focus

### Clustering Information

The product of a brainstorming activity is a set of ideas, but the ideas are not necessarily organized in the order in which they will appear in the final essay. **Clustering** is the process of grouping similar ideas to develop the information into a thesis statement, topic sentences, and supporting details.

A. Look at the first chart below. The writer has brainstormed ideas for a cause-and-effect essay. She has then eliminated irrelevant or problematic ideas. In the second chart, cluster her ideas using the categories provided.

| CAUSES ➤ | GROWTH SITUATION |
|---|---|
| listen to coach <br> a strong body <br> avoid injuries <br> fast decisions <br> cooperation with other players <br> ~~have lots of equipment~~ <br> being fast / agile <br> ~~a good diet~~ <br> stress management <br> supportive team player | becoming a successful professional athlete |

| MENTAL CLARITY | PHYSICAL STRENGTH | WORK WITH OTHERS |
|---|---|---|
| • _____ | • _____ | • _____ |
| • _____ | • _____ | • _____ |
| • _____ | • _____ | • _____ |

B. Look at your brainstorming ideas on page 133. Cluster your ideas into logical categories. Use the space below or a separate piece of paper.

## Exercise 7 Developing ideas into an outline

**Look at the outline elements below. Answer the questions that follow.**

| THESIS STATEMENT |
| --- |
| The factors that determine if an individual can have a successful career in professional sports include physical ability, mental clarity, and working well with others. |

| BODY PARAGRAPH 1 | BODY PARAGRAPH 2 | BODY PARAGRAPH 3 |
| --- | --- | --- |
| To become a professional athlete, a person must be athletically gifted.<br>• a strong body<br>• speed<br>• avoid injuries | Another factor that contributes to a successful career in sports is a strong mind.<br>• manage stress<br>• make fast strategic decisions | An athlete must work well with others.<br>• listen to the coach's advice<br>• support other team members<br>• cooperate with other players |

1. Read the thesis statement. According to the writer, what causes lead to success in professional sports? _____

_____

_____

2. How has the writer organized the body paragraphs? _____

_____

_____

3. What is the topic in body paragraph 1? _____

_____

_____

4. What is the topic in body paragraph 2? _____

_____

_____

5. What is the topic in body paragraph 3? _____

_____

_____

6. How do the details support the topic sentences?
   a. They provide descriptions.     b. They give facts and statistics.

## Exercise 8 Writing an outline

GO ONLINE

Review your brainstorming ideas and your freewriting exercise. Then go to the Web to print out an outline template for your essay.

### In Writing Process Step 3 you will . . .

- learn to use phrasal verbs to write about cause-and-effect relationships.
- write a first draft of your cause-and-effect essay.

## Exercise 1 Reading a student essay

Read the essay. Name three traits of a professional athlete that can also lead to success in life.

## Maybe Not a Professional Athlete, but Still a Success

At this moment, somewhere in the world a young boy is dreaming about becoming a famous soccer player. He has posters of famous soccer stars in his room, and every day he goes out to practice with his friends. He even cuts his hair in the same style as his favorite player. Thousands of young people feel the same as this boy. Only a few children actually become professional athletes, but all of them will learn valuable skills while they pursue their dream. The factors that determine if an individual can have a successful career in professional sports include physical ability, mental clarity, and the ability to work well with others.

To become a professional athlete, a person must stay healthy and physically strong. A soccer star should be able to run faster and farther than most other athletes. A basketball player has to be able to fake, block, and shoot while other powerful players are trying to stop him. Athletes need the support of their families. Finally, to make a career of sports, the player must be able to avoid injuries. Many young athletes have to quit because they have sports injuries from playing year after year. So a powerful, agile, and resilient body is essential.

Another factor that contributes to a successful career in sports is a strong mind. An athlete must be able to manage stress and focus on the game. A tennis player might feel a lot of stress, which could interfere with her ability to concentrate. She might hit the ball out of bounds. A crowd of people yelling at a baseball pitcher might make him throw balls instead of strikes. To succeed, an athlete must be able to play under this kind of pressure. Athletes need the right kind of equipment to perform at their peak. In addition, an athlete must be able to make quick, strategic decisions. Making the right decision to pass or shoot, for example, is extremely important, especially in team sports.

Finally, an athlete must be able to cooperate with his team members. So even though he might want to keep the ball and make all the shots, he must focus on passing the ball to the player who has the best chance of scoring. He must follow and trust his coach's strategies for the team, even if it means he will not score the winning shot. He must understand his teammates' abilities and know who is the fastest player and who is the most accurate. He cannot think only about himself if he wants his team to win.

In conclusion, the three contributing factors to a successful career in athletics are physical ability, mental clarity, and the ability to work well with others. Not all children will become professional athletes, but these skills will be valuable to them later in their lives. Staying healthy will help them grow and live longer lives. Developing a strong mind will help them do well in school and in careers. And if they learn to work well with others, they will get along well with colleagues and friends.

## Exercise 2 Examining the student essay

**Examine the organization of the essay by responding to the questions and statements below. Compare your answers with a partner.**

1. Underline the hook. Which of the following strategies is used?
   a. a short story          b. a surprising statement          c. a famous quote

2. What background information do you learn in the first paragraph?

   _____

   _____

3. Circle and label the thesis statement.

4. According to the thesis statement, how many main causes will be discussed?
   What are they? _____

5. Underline and label the topic sentence of each body paragraph.

6. Draw a line through any sentences that do not support the topic sentence of that paragraph.

7. Does the author restate the thesis statement in the conclusion? _____

8. What type of comment does the writer make in the conclusion?
   a. a warning          b. advice          c. a prediction

## Using Phrasal Verbs when Discussing Causes and Effects

**Phrasal verbs** are a combination of a verb + other words (often a preposition) that gives a specific meaning of an action. Sometimes following a verb with a different preposition can dramatically change its meaning.

**Break up** (to separate into many pieces)
The spaceship **broke up** as it entered the atmosphere.

**Break down** (stop working)
The car **broke down** on the road.

Here are some phrasal verbs you can use when you write about causes and effects.

| Phrasal Verbs | Examples |
|---|---|
| **decide to** + verb in base form | Masoud **decided to** study more. |
| **hope to** + verb in base form | Anjali **hoped to** learn something. |
| **set** (something) **in motion** or **set in motion** + noun or noun phrase | The changes **set** the discussion **in motion.** |
| **result in** + noun, noun phrase, or verb in gerund (-*ing*) form | The fight **resulted in** suffering. |
| **lead to** + noun, noun phrase, or verb in gerund (-*ing*) form | Malnutrition **leads to** sickness. |
| **try out** + noun, noun phrase, or verb in gerund (-*ing*) form | She **tried out** the new method. |
| **believe in** + noun, noun phrase, or verb in gerund (-*ing*) form | I **believe in** working hard. |
| **end in** + noun, noun phrase, or verb in gerund (-*ing*) form | The event **ended in** a meal. |

## Exercise 3 Using phrasal verbs

**A. Complete each sentence to demonstrate your understanding of the underlined phrasal verbs.**

1. Higher employment <u>results in</u> *increased spending.* _____

   _____

   _____

2. The huge storm <u>ended in</u> _____

   _____

   _____

3. The students <u>hoped to</u> _____

   _____

   _____

4. The new policies set <u>in motion</u> _____

   _____

   _____

5. Our neighbors <u>decided to</u> _____

   _____

   _____

**B. Write sentences for your essay using phrasal verbs.**

_____

_____

_____

_____

_____

_____

_____

_____

## Exercise 4 Writing a first draft

**GO ONLINE**

Review your outline. Then write the first draft of a cause-and-effect essay about how and why you or a person you know grew and changed over time in a specific way. Go to the Web to use the Online Writing Tutor.

## Exercise 5 Peer editing a first draft

A. After writing a first draft, it is helpful to get feedback on your ideas. Exchange essays with two other people. For each essay you read, answer the Peer Editor's Questions on a separate piece of paper. Then discuss your responses.

**GO ONLINE**

## Peer Editor's Questions

1. What is your favorite part of the essay?

2. What effect does the writer introduce in the background information?

3. What causes does the writer present?

4. What parts of the essay could be supported with more details?

5. Is there any information in the essay that does not support the writer's thesis?

6. Why is this topic important to the writer? How do you know?

**Go to the Web to print out a peer editor's worksheet.**

B. Review your feedback and the organization guidelines on page 135. Make notes for your revision. In this step, you may add, remove, or rewrite information to clarify your ideas.

### In **Writing Process Step 4** you will . . .

- learn about the use of future with *will*.
- learn about using *will* with *so that*.
- learn about future possibility with *if* clauses.
- edit your first draft and write a second draft.

Now that you have written a first draft, it is time to edit. Editing involves making changes to your writing to improve it and to correct mistakes.

GO ONLINE

## Language and Grammar Focus

### The Future with *Will*

In a cause-and-effect essay, you will need to discuss future effects of a cause or set of causes. The **modal** *will* is often used to talk about the future.

Use *will* to make predictions. You can also use adverbs like *probably* or *certainly* with *will* to express a degree of certainty.

> He **will win** the race.
> He **will** <u>probably</u> **be** wealthy one day.

*Will* is followed by the base form of the verb.

Use the same form of *will* with any subject.

| FUTURE WITH *WILL* | | | |
|---|---|---|---|
| **SUBJECT** | ***WILL* (+ *NOT*)** | **BASE FORM OF THE VERB** | |
| I | | **be** | rich. |
| You | | | |
| She | **will** | **have** | success. |
| We | **will not** | | |
| You | | **save** | money. |
| They | | | |

## Exercise 1 Making predictions with *will*

Finish the following sentences to make predictions. Use *will* or *will not*.

1. A talented actor <u>will probably become famous.</u> _____

   _____

2. A hardworking student _____

   _____

3. A dedicated employee _____

   _____

4. An overworked and exhausted doctor _____

_____

5. An employee who has a lot of personal problems _____

_____

GO ONLINE

## Language and Grammar Focus

### Using *Will* with *So That*

The future with *will* can also be used with the logical connector *so that*. In this type of sentence, the main clause uses the simple present and states the cause. It is followed by *so that* and a second main clause with *will*.

| main clause (present) | | time clause (future) |
|---|---|---|
| Students work hard in school | **so that** | they **will be** successful. |

## Exercise 2 Using *will* with *so that*

**Rewrite the sentences below using *so that* and *will*.**

1. Some drivers drink a lot of caffeinated drinks to stay awake.

   *Some drivers drink a lot of caffeinated drinks so that they will*
   *stay awake.*

2. Students sacrifice many things to save money for school.

   _____

   _____

3. Many stores advertise sales to attract customers.

   _____

   _____

4. Many people pay bills online to save money and time.

   _____

   _____

5. Some people carpool to work to save money.

   _____

   _____

**GO ONLINE**

## Language and Grammar Focus

### Expressing Future Possibility With *If* Clauses

Sentences with an *if* clause show a cause-and-effect relationship. The *if* clause introduces a possible situation (the cause). The main clause talks about the possible result (the effect) of the situation.

Use the simple present in the *if* clause and *will* in the main clause.

| cause | effect |
|---|---|

**If** X happens, Y **will happen**, too.

The cause-and-effect clauses can come in either order. When the *if* clause comes first, it is followed by a comma.

| *if* clause | | main clause |
|---|---|---|

**If** Pedro plays,      we **will win** the game.

| main clause | | *if* clause |
|---|---|---|

We **will win** the game      **if** Pedro plays.

> **!** Do not use *will* in the *if* clause.
>
> **X**    If the price of oil will increase, people will drive less. (INCORRECT)
>
>      If the price of oil increases, people will drive less.

## Exercise 3 Forming *if* clauses

**Combine the ideas below so that they form one sentence with an *if* clause.**

1. (money managers / be discipline / achieve financial goals)

   *If money managers are disciplined, they will achieve financial goals.*

   _____

2. (applicant / interview well / receive job offers)

   _____

   _____

3. (you / exercise regularly / be healthy in old age)

   _____

   _____

4. (restaurant / serve delicious food / be successful)

_____

_____

5. (I / work hard / be promoted)

_____

_____

6. (parents / be good at solving problems / be successful at raising children.)

_____

_____

## Exercise 4 Editing a paragraph

**Read the paragraph, and edit as necessary. There are five mistakes in verb form and one mistake in punctuation.**

If people continue to choose to move from small towns into cities for greater opportunities, cities will have to adapt to the changes in their populations. Cities will need to create more affordable housing for new residents. They are need to build schools for their children so that they will study, and parks so that they will play. Transportation and other services will needing to be expanded to accommodate larger numbers of people. If the city meets this challenge people will be able to move to and from their jobs easily. If it does not, people probably earn less money, as they will only be able to accept work that is close to their homes. As cities expand, new neighborhoods will being created in areas that are now uninhabited. Areas that were once considered suburban will most probably be swallowed up by urban expansion and become part of the city. As new neighborhoods are established, new businesses will also open to meet the needs of these new residents. With these new businesses are coming new jobs.

## Exercise 5 Editing your first draft and rewriting

Review your essay for mistakes. Use the checklist below. Then write a final draft.
Go to the Web to use the Online Writing Tutor.

GO ONLINE

### Editor's Checklist

**Put a check (✓) as appropriate.**

**CONTENT AND ORGANIZATION**

○ 1. Does your introduction include a hook to get the reader's attention?

○ 2. Do your background sentences describe the result of the causes?

○ 3. Does each body paragraph have a topic sentence that states one cause mentioned in your thesis statement?

○ 4. Does your conclusion summarize the causes and discuss other possible effects of the event?

**LANGUAGE**

○ 5. Did you use correct verb tenses?

○ 6. Did you follow the rules for using *will* correctly?

○ 7. Did you use *so that* to show cause-and-effect relationships?

○ 8. Did you use *if* clauses to show cause-and-effect?

○ 9. Did you check the punctuation?

**Go to the Web to print out a peer editor's worksheet.**

### In **Review** you will . . .

- practice using phrasal verbs.
- review making predictions with *will*.
- practice using *will* with *so that*.
- practice forming *if* clauses.

In Putting It All Together you will review what you learned in this unit.

## Exercise 1 Using phrasal verbs

**Fill in the blank with the correct preposition. Use *in*, *out*, or *to*.**

1. The man decided _____ take the job.

2. Economists often hope _____ predict what will happen to the economy.

3. The successful job interview resulted _____ a new professional opportunity.

4. The new elections had set _____ motion the change that came afterward.

5. She had moved to the city because she wanted to try _____ life in a new place.

## Exercise 2 Making predictions with *will*

**Complete the following sentences with a prediction. Use *will* or *will not*.**

1. A person who wants to lose weight _____

   _____

2. A terrible teacher _____

   _____

3. A careful driver _____

   _____

4. A vegetarian _____

   _____

5. A dishonest salesperson _____

   _____

6. A successful politician _____

   _____

7. A person who wants to be a millionaire _____

   _____

## Exercise 3 Using *will* with *so that*

**Rewrite the sentences below using *will* and *so that*.**

1. Many people exercise to be healthy.

   _____

   _____

2. Many nurses wear special shoes to be comfortable.

   _____

   _____

3. Many immigrants work hard to be successful in their new country.

   _____

   _____

4. Many homeowners have alarm systems to feel safe.

   _____

   _____

5. Many older people have pets to not feel lonely.

   _____

   _____

6. Many schools offer financial aid to attract new students.

   _____

   _____

7. Many people work very hard to be successful.

   _____

   _____

8. Many workplaces provide coffee to keep workers awake.

   _____

   _____

9. Many hikers carry poles to keep their balance.

   _____

   _____

## Exercise 4 Forming *if* clauses

**Combine the ideas below so that they form one sentence with an *if* clause.**

1. (a person / work as an international pilot / travel to other countries)

   _____

   _____

2. (you / learn another language / feel a sense of accomplishment)

   _____

   _____

3. (you / have good computer skills / be qualified for many good jobs)

   _____

   _____

4. (a person / respect others / have a lot of friends)

   _____

   _____

5. (you / plan your vacation carefully / have fewer problems during your trip)

   _____

   _____

6. (she / invest money wisely / become wealthy)

   _____

   _____

7. (students / study hard / graduate college)

   _____

   _____

8. (athletes / train regularly / win medals)

   _____

   _____

9. (you / read a lot / improve your vocabulary)

   _____

   _____

## Exercise 5 Editing a paragraph

**Read the paragraph, and edit as necessary. There are six mistakes with future verb forms and *if* clauses.**

Children who participate in sports will be more successful in their jobs. First of all, team sports require kids to play together with their team. In this way, they will to learn cooperation skills. For example, while playing soccer, a child might realize that a teammate has a better chance of scoring a goal. If he will pass the ball to his teammate, he will not control it anymore. However, his teammate will probably score a goal. By learning to cooperate on the playing field, the child will one day be a more efficient employee. In addition, children who play team sports will learning how to be good sports. If the team will lose a game, the child remembers that it is only a game. Instead of getting upset, he will to try to do better next time. And when he works for a company, he will not to get upset if he loses an important client or sale.

 In **Timed Writing** you will . . .

- practice writing with a time limit.

Practice your test-taking skills with the following practice topic. Read the prompt. Then follow the steps below.

> Very few people live in the same home their entire lives. What causes people to move to new homes either in the same city or in different parts of the world?

## Step 1  BRAINSTORMING: 5 minutes

Write ideas and vocabulary for your essay on a separate piece of paper. You may want to cluster your ideas.

## Step 2  OUTLINING: 5 minutes

Write an outline for your essay. Use another piece of paper if necessary.

| **Introduction (First Paragraph)** | |
| --- | --- |
| **Hook**<br>Get your reader interested. | |
| **Background Information**<br>Explain the effect. | |
| **Thesis Statement**<br>Present the causes. | |
| **Body Paragraphs (Middle Paragraphs)** | |
| **Topic Sentences**<br>Present one cause in each paragraph.<br>Provide details. | |
| **Supporting Sentences**<br>Explain each cause. | |
| **Conclusion (Last Paragraph)** | |
| **Restatement and Comment**<br>Restate your thesis in new words.<br>Present some future effects. | |

**WRITING: 40 MINUTES**

Use your brainstorming notes and outline to write your essay on a separate piece of paper.

**EDITING: 10 MINUTES**

When you have finished your essay, check it for mistakes. Use this checklist.

GO ONLINE

## Editor's Checklist

**Put a check (✓) as appropriate.**

○ 1. Does the introduction include a hook and background information that explains the effect of the causes?

○ 2. Is there a thesis statement that focuses the essay? Does it mention what causes people to move to new places?

○ 3. Does each body paragraph have a topic sentence that states one cause mentioned in the thesis statement?

○ 4. Do supporting sentences in each body paragraph explain the cause in the topic sentence of that paragraph?

○ 5. Does the conclusion summarize the causes and comment on them?

○ 6. Did you follow the rules for using *will* correctly?

○ 7. Did you use *if* clauses to show cause and/or effect?

**Go to the Web to print out a peer editor's worksheet.**

**Test-Taking Tip**

Read the last line of every paragraph, and make sure it is logically connected to the first sentence of the following paragraph.

**Write a cause-and-effect essay on one of the following topics.**

**Dietary Health:** Many people claim that the way we eat is not as healthy as it was in the past. They say that the way food is produced is harmful for the environment and to people's health. Discuss several ways in which food is produced, sold, and prepared differently than in the past. How have these changes affected the environment and human health?

**Early Education:** Increasingly, countries are paying more attention to early education programs. Formal early childhood education programs are becoming more prevalent and accessible. In some countries these programs are even required. What is causing countries to focus attention on these programs?

**Environmental Science:** There has been much discussion recently about global warming. What are some of the causes of climate change? Do humans have the power to stop global warming?

**Gerontology:** In the 21st century, we have access to new techniques and knowledge that allow people to live longer. Discuss several reasons why people now routinely live into their 70s and 80s and may live well beyond that.

**Information Technology (IT):** Often people say that the world has gotten "smaller." They do not mean physically smaller but that communication across distances is now easier, and people feel closer. In the past, if a person moved to another country, it was entirely possible that he or she would never again speak with the friends and family left behind. Now this situation is dramatically different. What are some specific inventions of the last century that have contributed to this change?

**Psychology:** There are many reasons for psychological disorders, and especially in the case of some particular pathologies, there is much debate surrounding their causes. What are some of the possible causes of psychological disorders?

# Appendices

## Step 1: Stimulating Ideas

Begin writing by gathering ideas. Read your assignment carefully, and make sure you understand the task. Then think about what you already know about the topic.

▶ **Strategies:** Highlight important parts of your assignment. Talk to classmates about your ideas, and write about them in your journal. Circle the ideas that are the most interesting to you. Then choose one to write about.

## Step 2: Brainstorming and Outlining

Make a plan that has a clear focus and a logical sequence. To write in a way that the reader will understand, organize your ideas into an introduction, body paragraphs, and a conclusion.

▶ **Strategies:** Create a list, diagram, chart, or web. Use it to decide how you will organize your essay. Think about your audience and purpose as you organize. Also make a list of vocabulary words that you think you will use. Check your assignment again to be sure your plan matches the assignment. Finally, make an outline that will guide your drafting process.

## Step 3: Developing Your Ideas

Write a first draft that explains your ideas. Try to follow the outline, and explain the ideas as clearly as you can. You may change your ideas as you write to better support your thesis and to add details.

▶ **Strategies:** Review your assignment before you write your first draft. Double space so that you have room to make changes later. When you finish, reread your work. Add connectors to make your ideas flow more effectively, remove anything that does not support your thesis, and add details that will make your writing clearer. Have a peer read your paper and give you feedback.

## Step 4: Editing Your Writing

Your second draft and sometimes third draft give you opportunities to clarify your meaning and check grammar, vocabulary, spelling, and punctuation. The final draft should be easy to read and should have no mistakes.

▶ **Strategies:** Use a checklist to look for mistakes in subject-verb agreement, verb tense, singular/plural forms, word forms, word order, and punctuation. Also check a dictionary for any vocabulary or spelling questions you have. Then write a final draft. Make sure this final draft has one-inch margins, is double spaced, has a title, and lists your name, date, and class on the top of the first page.

## Commas

A comma (,) is used to separate information from other parts of the sentence.

1. A comma is used to separate items in a series. Use *and* before the last item if listing three or more items.
   - We made rice, chicken, salad, and cake.

2. A comma is used to separate an introductory word or phrase.
   - At the end of the day, my husband and I sit on the sofa and talk.

3. A comma is used after a dependent clause when the dependent clause precedes (or introduces) an independent clause.
   - When the power went off, we could not listen to the radio.

4. A comma is used to separate two main clauses when there is a conjunction such as *and, but,* or *so* that shows a relationship between the clauses.
   - The temperature was below freezing, but we were warm.

5. A comma is used to separate an appositive from the rest of the sentence. An appositive appearing after any noun in a sentence is set off with commas.
   - We used to visit Miraflores, a beach community near Lima.
   - The speaker, an Ecuadorian economist, supported his points with facts and statistics.

## Periods

Periods (.) are used to mark the end of a sentence.
- She speaks four languages.

## Colons

Colons (:) are used to introduce a list of items. They can be particularly helpful when writing thesis statements because they allow the writer to introduce the major ideas.

Colons must be preceded by an independent clause. They can be followed by a group of words, phrases or, in some cases, clauses.
- To build a tree house, you will need the following items: nails, a hammer, boards, and a tape measure.

## Semicolons

Semicolons (;) are used at the end of sentences. They follow the same rules as periods; however, they are only appropriate if the relationship between the two sentences is close.

1. Semicolons are used between two separate sentences.

   - They help each other; Emily does the bookkeeping while Amina takes care of customers.

2. Semicolons are used when two sentences are joined by a connector such as *however* or *therefore*.

   - The Earth's oceans still hold many secrets; however, new technology is helping scientists to understand them better.

## Apostrophes

Apostrophes (') are used to show possession.

1. When a noun is singular, add an apostrophe and *s* to show possession. In the first example, the writer has one cousin.

   - We went to my cousin's house.

2. When a noun is plural, put the apostrophe after the plural *s*. In the next example, the writer has more than one cousin.

   - We went to my cousins' house.

3. When a noun ends in *s*, you may add the apostrophe + *s* after the final *s* or just the apostrophe.

   - My boss's car was ridiculously expensive.
   - My boss' car was ridiculously expensive.

Apostrophes are also used in contractions. (Note, however, that contractions are not appropriate in most academic writing.)

   - Scott doesn't have any hair.

## Quotation Marks

Quotation marks ("...") are used to show that you are repeating or quoting someone else's words.

Put quotation marks around only the exact words you take from someone else's speech or writing. Use a comma to separate the quote from the rest of the sentence.

- I heard him say, "Don't worry about the report, Mr. Noor. I will take care of it."

## GIVING EXAMPLES

| CONNECTORS | EXAMPLES |
|---|---|
| *for example*<br>*for instance* | • My best friend is so loyal; **for example,** she flies to Mali every year to visit me.<br>• The Polish language is grammatically quite different from English. **For instance,** it does not have articles. |

## SHOWING CONTRAST

| CONNECTORS | EXAMPLES |
|---|---|
| *but*<br>*yet*<br>*whereas*<br>*even though*<br>*although*<br>*however*<br>*in contrast*<br>*unlike* | • I wanted to talk to her, **but** I was afraid she would not like me.<br>• He never finished college, **yet** he became a millionaire at the age of 25.<br>• **Whereas** many large cats are almost extinct, the number of African lions is on the rise across the continent.<br>• **Even though** he did not attend school, he taught himself to read and write.<br>• **Although** the Guggenheim museum has a modern appearance, it fits into the old architecture of New York City very well.<br>• We expected good weather; **however,** it rained very hard all day.<br>• I have seven siblings; **in contrast,** my husband is an only child.<br>• **Unlike** Mexican tortillas, Spanish tortillas are made with eggs. |

## GIVING REASONS

| CONNECTORS | EXAMPLES |
|---|---|
| *so*<br>*because* | • I was distracted by the stars, **so** I didn't see the big puddle.<br>• I used to eat a lot of fish **because** we lived next to the ocean. |

## SHOWING RESULTS

| CONNECTORS | EXAMPLES |
|---|---|
| *therefore*<br>*consequently* | • He did not want to be late; **therefore,** he took an earlier train than usual.<br>• Our house was on a small hill; **consequently,** we were safe during the flood. |

## ADDING INFORMATION

| CONNECTORS | EXAMPLES |
|---|---|
| *and*<br>*in addition*<br>*moreover* | • The hotel was built on a cliff, **and** it had marvelous views of the ocean.<br>• Deforestation poses a threat to many native species. **In addition,** the construction of a large factory in the area is causing great environmental damage.<br>• We were lost in the forest; **moreover,** it was getting dark. |

## SHOWING SIMILARITIES

| CONNECTORS | EXAMPLES |
|---|---|
| *similarly*<br>*likewise*<br>*like* | • Hollywood makes a variety of movies that are distributed around the world; **similarly,** Mumbai makes movies for international export.<br>• Binh started working for his father; **likewise,** his brother began working there at the age of 22. |

## SHOWING TIME RELATIONSHIPS

| CONNECTORS | EXAMPLES |
|---|---|
| *while*<br>*when*<br>*before*<br>*after*<br>*after that*<br>*meanwhile*<br>*then*<br>*finally* | • I listen to the radio **while** I chat online.<br>• We were getting ready to go to my grandfather's house **when** my father's friends showed up.<br>• **Before** the game began, the umpire flipped a coin.<br>• **After** I count the money and put it in the safe, I can close the store and go home.<br>• I count the money and put it in the safe. **After that,** I can close the store and go home.<br>• Bring the water to a boil. **Meanwhile,** chop the vegetables.<br>• Add salt and **then** stir carefully until it has fully dissolved. **Finally,** heat the mixture to 50 degrees Celsius. |

## DRAWING CONCLUSIONS

| CONNECTORS | EXAMPLES |
|---|---|
| *in conclusion*<br>*in summary* | • **In conclusion,** there are surprising similarities in these two architects' use of building materials.<br>• Unemployment is very high. Interest rates are going up, and the rate of inflation is on the increase. **In summary,** the economic reforms do not seem to be working. |

Adapted from the **Grammar Sense** *Glossary of Grammar Terms*

**action verb** A verb that describes a thing that someone or something does. An action verb does not describe a state or condition.

> Sam **rang** the bell.
>
> It **rains** a lot here.

**active sentence** In active sentences, the agent (the noun that is performing the action) is in subject position, and the receiver (the noun that receives or is a result of the action) is in object position. In the following sentence, the subject *Alex* performed the action, and the object *letter* received the action.

> Alex mailed the letter.

**adjective** A word that describes or modifies the meaning of a noun.

> the **orange** car          a **strange** noise

**adverb** A word that describes or modifies the meaning of a verb, another adverb, an adjective, or a sentence. Many adverbs answer such questions as *How? When? Where?* or *How often?* They often end in *-ly*.

> She ran **quickly**.          She ran **very** quickly.
>
> a **really** hot day          **Maybe** she'll leave.

**adverbial phrase** A phrase that functions as an adverb.

> Claudia spoke **very softly**.

**affirmative statement** A sentence that does not have a negative verb.

> Linda went to the movies.

**agreement** The subject and verb of a clause must agree in number. If the subject is singular, the verb form is also singular. If the subject is plural, the verb form is also plural.

> **He comes** home early.     **They come** home early.

**article** The words *a, an,* and *the* in English. Articles are used to introduce and identify nouns.

> **a** potato     **an** onion     **the** supermarket

**auxiliary verb** A verb that is used before main verbs (or other auxiliary verbs) in a sentence. Auxiliary verbs are usually used in questions and negative sentences. *Do, have,* and *be* can act as auxiliary verbs. Modals (*may, can, will . . .*) are also auxiliary verbs.

> **Do** you have the time?     The car **was** speeding.
>
> I **have** never been to Italy.     I **may** be late.

**base form** The form of a verb without any verb endings; the infinitive form without *to*.

> sleep     be     stop

**clause** A group of words that has a subject and a verb. *See also* **dependent clause** and **main clause.**

> If I leave, . . .          . . . when he speaks.
>
> The rain stopped.          . . . that I saw.

**common noun** A noun that refers to any of a class of people, animals, places, things, or ideas. Common nouns are not capitalized.

> man     cat     city     pencil     grammar

**comparative** A form of an adjective, adverb, or noun that is used to express differences between two items or situations.

> This book is **heavier than** that one.
>
> He runs more **quickly than** his brother.
>
> The DVD costs **more money than** the CD.

**complex sentence** A sentence that has a main clause and one or more dependent clauses.

> When the bell rang, we were finishing dinner.

**compound sentence** A sentence that has two main clauses separated by a comma and a conjunction, or by a semi-colon.

> She is very talented; she can sing and dance.

**conditional sentence** A sentence that expresses a real or unreal situation in the *if* clause, and the (real or unreal) expected result in the main clause.

> If I have time, I will travel to Africa.
>
> If I had time, I would travel to Africa.

**count noun** A common noun that can be counted. It usually has both a singular and a plural form.

> orange — oranges          woman — women

**definite article** The word *the* in English. It is used to identify nouns based on assumptions about what information the speaker and listener share about the noun. The definite article is also used for making general statements about a whole class or group of nouns.

> Please give me **the** key.
>
> **The** scorpion is dangerous.

**dependent clause** A clause that cannot stand alone as a sentence because it depends on the main clause to complete the meaning of the sentence. Also called *subordinate clause.*

> I'm going home **after he calls**.

**determiner** A word such as *a, an, the, this, that, these, those, my, some, a few,* and all numbers used before a noun to limit its meaning in some way.

> **those** videos

**future** A time that is to come. The future is expressed in English with *will, be going to,* the simple present, or the present continuous. These different forms of the future often have different meanings and uses.

> I **will** help you later.
>
> David **is going to** call later.
>
> The train **leaves** at 6:05 this evening.
>
> **I'm driving** to Toronto tomorrow.

**gerund** An *-ing* form of a verb that is used in place of a noun or pronoun to name an activity or a state.

> **Skiing** is fun.　　　He doesn't like **being sick.**

**if clause** A dependent clause that begins with *if* and expresses a real or unreal situation.

> **If I have the time,** I'll paint the kitchen.
>
> **If I had the time,** I'd paint the kitchen.

**indefinite article** The words *a* and *an* in English. Indefinite articles introduce a noun as a member of a class of nouns or make generalizations about a whole class or group of nouns.

> **An** ocean is **a** large body of water.

**independent clause** *See* **main clause.**

**indirect object** A noun or pronoun used after some verbs that refers to the person who receives the direct object of a sentence.

> Hassan wrote a letter to **Samuel.**
>
> Please buy some milk for **us.**

**infinitive** A verb form that includes *to* + the base form of a verb. An infinitive is used in place of a noun or pronoun to name an activity or situation expressed by a verb.

> Do you like **to swim?**

**intransitive verb** A verb that cannot be followed by an object.

> We finally **arrived.**

**main clause** A clause that can be used by itself as a sentence. Also called *independent clause.*

> **I'm going home.**

**main verb** A verb that can be used alone in a sentence. A main verb can also occur with an auxiliary verb.

> I **ate** lunch at 11:30.
>
> Kate can't **eat** lunch today.

**modal** The auxiliary verbs *can, could, may, might, must, should, will,* and *would.* They modify the meaning of a main verb by expressing ability, authority, formality, politeness, or various degrees of certainty. Also called *modal auxiliary.*

> You **should** take something for your headache.
>
> Applicants **must** have a high school diploma.

**negative statement** A sentence with a negative verb.

> I **didn't see** that movie.

**noun** A word that typically refers to a person, animal, place, thing, or idea.

> Tom　　　　　　　rabbit
>
> store　　　　　　　computer
>
> mathematics

**noun clause** A dependent clause that can occur in the same place as a noun, pronoun, or noun phrase in a sentence. Noun clauses begin with *wh–* words, *if, whether,* or *that.*

> I don't know **where he is.**
>
> I wonder **if he's coming.**
>
> I don't know **whether it's true.**
>
> I think **that it's a lie.**

**noun phrase** A phrase formed by a noun and its modifiers. A noun phrase can substitute for a noun in a sentence.

> She drank **milk.**
>
> She drank **chocolate milk.**
>
> She drank **the milk.**

**object** A noun, pronoun, or noun phrase that follows a transitive verb or a preposition.

> He likes **pizza.**　　　Go with **her.**
>
> She likes **tennis.**　　　Steve threw **the ball.**

**passive sentence** Passive sentences emphasize the receiver of an action by changing the usual order of the subject and object in a sentence. In the sentence below, the subject (*The letter*) does not perform the action; it receives the action or is the result of an action. The passive is formed with a form of *be* + the past participle of a transitive verb.

> The letter was mailed yesterday.

**past continuous** A verb form that expresses an action or situation in progress at a specific time in the past. The past continuous is formed with *was* or *were* + verb + *–ing.* Also called *past progressive.*

> A: What **were** you **doing** last night at eight o'clock?
>
> B: I **was studying.**

**past participle** A past verb form that may differ from the simple past form of some irregular verbs. It is used to form the present perfect.

> I have never **seen** that movie.

**phrasal verb** A two- or three-word verb such as *turn down* or *run out of*. The meaning of a phrasal verb is usually different from the meanings of its individual words.

> She **turned down** the job offer.
>
> Don't **run out of** gas on the freeway.

**phrase** A group of words that can form a grammatical unit. A phrase can take the form of a noun phrase, verb phrase, adjective phrase, adverbial phrase, or prepositional phrase. This means it can act as a noun, verb, adjective, adverb, or preposition.

> The **tall man** left.   She spoke **too fast.**
>
> Lee **hit the ball.**   They ran **down the stairs.**

**preposition** A word such as *at, in, on,* or *to* that links nouns, pronouns, and gerunds to other words.

**prepositional phrase** A phrase that consists of a preposition followed by a noun or noun phrase.

> on Tuesday            under the table

**present continuous** A verb form that indicates that an activity is in progress, temporary, or changing. It is formed with *be* + verb + *–ing.* Also called *present progressive.*

> I**'m watering** the garden.
>
> Ruth **is working** for her uncle.

**present perfect** A verb form that expresses a connection between the past and the present. It indicates indefinite past time, recent past time, or continuing past time. The present perfect is formed with *have* + the past participle of the main verb.

> I**'ve seen** that movie.
>
> The manager **has** just **resigned.**
>
> We**'ve been** here for three hours.

**pronoun** A word that can replace a noun or noun phrase. *I, you, he, she, it, mine,* and *yours* are some examples of pronouns.

**quantity expression** A word or words that occur before a noun to express a quantity or amount of that noun.

> **a lot of** rain            **few** books
> **four** trucks

**simple past** A verb form that expresses actions and situations that were completed at a definite time in the past.

> Kwon **ate** lunch.            She **was** hungry.

**simple present** A verb form that expresses general statements, especially about habitual or repeated activities and permanent situations.

> Every morning I **catch** the 8:00 bus.
>
> The Earth **is** round.

**stative verb** A type of verb that is not usually used in the continuous form because it expresses a condition or state that is not changing. *Know, love, see,* and *smell* are some examples.

**subject** A noun, pronoun, or noun phrase that precedes the verb phrase in a sentence. The subject is closely related to the verb as the doer or experiencer of the action or state, or closely related to the noun that is being described in a sentence with *be.*

> **Riko** kicked the ball.
> **The park** is huge.

**subordinate clause** *See* **dependent clause.**

**superlative** A form of an adjective, adverb, or noun that is used to rank an item or situation first or last in a group of three or more.

> This perfume has **the strongest** scent.
>
> He speaks **the fastest** of all.
>
> That machine makes **the most noise** of the three.

**tense** The form of a verb that shows past, present, and future time.

> He **lives** in Ankara now.
>
> He **lived** in Istanbul two years ago.
>
> He**'ll live** in Malatya next year.

**time clause** A dependent clause that begins with a word such as *while, when, before,* or *after.* It expresses the relationship in time between two different events in the same sentence.

> **Before Sandy left,** she fixed the copy machine.

**time expression** A phrase that functions as an adverb of time.

> She graduated **three years ago.**
>
> I'll see them **the day after tomorrow.**

**transitive verb** A verb that is followed by an object.

> I **read** the book.

**uncountable (noncount) noun** A common noun that cannot be counted. A noncount noun has no plural form and cannot occur with *a, an,* or a number.

> information      mathematics      weather

**verb** A word that refers to an action or a state.

> Thana **closed** the window.
> Tsutomu **loves** classical music.

**verb phrase** A phrase that has a main verb and any objects, adverbs, or dependent clauses that complete the meaning of the verb in the sentence.

> Who **called you?**
> He **walked slowly.**

| EFFECTIVE ACADEMIC WRITING 2: THE SHORT ESSAY | GRAMMAR SENSE 2 |
|---|---|
| **UNIT 2**<br>Adjectives in Descriptive Writing<br>Formation of Adjectives<br>Order of Adjectives | **CHAPTER 16**<br>Adjectives |
| **UNIT 3**<br>The Past Continuous in Narrative Essays<br>Past Time Clauses | **CHAPTER 5**<br>The Past Continuous and Past Time Clauses |
| **UNIT 4**<br>Comparatives in Comparison-Contrast Essays<br>Comparatives in Sentences | **CHAPTER 18**<br>Comparatives |
| **UNIT 5**<br>Quantity Expressions in Opinion Essays | **CHAPTER 14**<br>Nouns and Quantity Expressions |
| **UNIT 6**<br>Phrasal Verbs when Discussing Causes and Effects<br>The Future with *Will*<br>*Will* with *So That*<br>Future Possibilities with *If* Clauses | **CHAPTER 7**<br>Future Time: *Be Going To, Will,* and the Present Continuous<br><br>**CHAPTER 8**<br>Future Time Clauses and *If* Clauses |